TABLE OF CONTENTS

Dr. Tim Adams

Foundational Doctrines of the Christian Faith

God

Christ

Holy Spirit

Satan

Man

Salvation

Church

Bible

Prayer

Prophecy

"That we henceforth be no more children, tossed to and fro, and carried about with every wind of doctrine, by the sleight of men, and cunning craftiness, whereby they lie in wait to deceive."

Ephesians 4:14

Foundational Doctrines of

the Christian Faith

All Scripture quotations are from the
King James Version of the Bible
unless otherwise stated.

Printed in the United States of America
by Shepherd's Voice Ministries.

Cover Design: Tim Adams and Eric Beaty

Preface

Doctrine is boring! That is the common misperception of many in the Church. You might think you prefer to study something that will help you with your marriage, with other relationships, with your children, with your work, with your finances, with direction and purpose in your life. Those things are certainly important. Scripture has much to say about all those things, but consider an example that makes a strong case for doctrinal study in the believer's life.

The cement slab your house sits on may be boring, too. It's basically a small parking lot with a house on it. How boring is that? That cement slab may not be as exciting as the kitchen cabinets, the wood paneling, the decorative moldings, ceiling fixtures, the carpet, the appliances you set on top of it in your house. However, without that boring cement slab, you cannot build anything that will last. Without that foundation, none of these more interesting, more exciting, seemingly more useful things can even stand at all. It's like the man who built his house on the rock, versus the man who built his house on the sand. Those beautiful kitchen cabinets sink in the sand, and they wash away, without the boring old cement slab. The beautiful walls, the nice staircase, crack and crumble without that boring, old cement slab.

We need to develop an appreciation for the foundational truths, the doctrines of our faith, because without them, none of the seemingly more interesting, more exciting things, more applicable things in our Christian lives can stand on anything solid and sure. Without the foundational truths of our faith, nothing in our lives finds a prosperous footing. What we're looking at is an essential part of the whole building, the foundation; and God seeks to build a faith perspective in every area of our experience.

Foundations of the Christian Faith can be used in small group studies or taught in a congregational setting. These eleven lessons may be divided into multiple sessions. The study is geared for interactive discussion. My prayer is that Christian doctrine will overcome its boring reputation.

Dr. Tim Adams

Acknowledgments

I thank God for moving my heart to teach the rudimentary doctrines of the Christian faith in all seven churches that I've pastored. I also thank Him for moving the hearts of my flock to thoroughly enjoy doctrinal studies. I continue to thank God for mature saints who are exercised in doctrinal truth, thereby producing dependable servants in the kingdom of God.

My wife has truly been God's gift to me in the ministry. She has always been encouraging to God's leadership in my life for whatever direction the teaching ministry has taken. Her love and support has been nothing less than extraordinary and humbling to my heart.

Eric Beaty is my friend. God sent him to me for such a time as this in my ministry. He spent countless hours walking me through the steps to book publishing. Without Eric I would have to tackle the book covers on my own, something possible but certainly not wise. His input has been incredibly valuable, and reaffirms to my heart that real friends are worth more than gold. Thanks, Eric.

LESSON ONE
The Doctrine of God

LESSON TITLE: The Doctrine of God - Theology

SCRIPTURE: Genesis 1:1

TRUTH TO GAIN: The reality of God as given in Scripture demands unfaltering belief, utmost worship, and the absolute loyalty of man.

His Existence

The Bible does not try to prove the existence of God. The Bible simply accepts the existence of God. The very first verse of the Bible accepts the existence of God in just four words of the verse, **In the beginning God.** Then it says, **God created the heavens and the earth.** There would be no heavens and no earth without God, but where did God come from? When a child or a skeptic asks the question "where did God come from," they are asking the wrong question. It does not fit reality. That is like asking "what does blue smell like?" Blue is not in the category of things that smell. God is not in the category of things that are created and so to ask where He came from, what caused God, who created God, is to ask the nonsensical. God is God and He had no creator. Though His name appears in the first verse of Scripture after the word *beginning* there would have been no beginning if God had not been in existence before that beginning, because everything has its beginning from God. It is accurate to say He is the Uncaused Cause. The Bible says in Hebrews 7:3 that God came in the flesh in the form of His Son Jesus who was, **Without father, without mother, without descent, having neither beginning of days, nor end of life (Hebrews 7:3).** It is true to say that God never, never was and will never, ever cease to be.

Proverbs 14:1 says, **The fool hath said in his heart, There is no God.** Never a truer statement was made because you really would have to be a fool to say that statement, and here is why. The dictionary defines a fool as "someone who lacks judgment or sense, a weak-minded or idiotic person." That definition perfectly describes someone who says there is no God. The Bible never seeks to prove the existence of God because the Bible assumes that His creation would never be so deliberately stupid to say there is no God. The atheist Bertrand Russell wrote in his book *Why I am Not a Christian,* that if it is true that all things need a cause, then God must also need a cause. He concluded from this that if God needed a cause, then God was not God; and if God is not God, then of course there is no God–so the fool Bertrand Russell said. However, it is important for us in a study of the doctrine of God to examine the evidence for the existence of God. Though the Bible never seeks to prove the existence of God it constantly brags on the evidence there is for God.

There are three ways that the Scripture says that man can know the existence of God. First, there is **NATURAL OBSERVATION**. Romans 1:19-20 says,

> **Because that which may be known of God is manifest in them; for God hath showed it unto them. For the invisible things of him from the creation of the world are clearly seen, being understood by the things that are made, even his eternal power and Godhead; so that they are without excuse.**

Man can look at the order and design of the universe and clearly discover evidence for God as the Creator/Designer. Any man who says he cannot do that is blind, foolish, and without excuse according to this verse.

Secondly, you can know the existence of God through **DIVINE REVELATION.** In 2 Peter 3:16, the apostle is speaking of the scoffers and skeptics of the last days who just won't believe the Scriptures. Peter says,

> **As also in all his epistles, speaking in them of these things; in which are some things hard to be understood, which they that are unlearned and unstable wrest, as they do also the other scriptures, unto their own destruction (2 Peter 3:16).**

That word *wrest* is the Greek word *strebloo,* and it means to torture by twisting (like on a torture rack) or by perversion. There is nothing wrong with the Scriptures. They reveal God perfectly. The problem is with man and his perverted heart who wants to explain away God. When man does that he does it to his own destruction, Peter says,

The final way of perceiving the existence of God is by **SPIRITUAL INSPIRATION**. This takes things from head knowledge to heart knowledge. Natural observation will not get you to heaven. You can look at the sun, moon, stars, planets, trees, birds, and flowers all day long and admire the Creator's handiwork, but that is only the first step in Christian belief–a head knowledge that even the devils have and tremble. James 2:19 says, **Thou believest that there is one God; thou doest well: the devils also believe, and tremble.** Only the Spirit of God can bring you to a salvation experience with the one God who died for man. 1 Corinthians 2:19 says, **But the natural man receiveth not the things of the Spirit of God: for they are foolishness unto him: neither can he know them, because they are spiritually discerned.** There has to be a spiritual experience called the "new birth" for a person to claim salvation.

Christians need to know how to convince the rationalistic, skeptical mind of these days concerning the existence of God. Titus 1:9 says, **Holding fast the faithful word as he hath been taught, that he may be able by sound doctrine both to exhort and to convince the gainsayers.** When the polls say that 92% of Americans believe there is a God, but only 9% have a biblical world view; 33% believe in moral absolutes that do not change by circumstances; only 50% believe the Bible is accurate; over half - 53% of Christians believe you earn your salvation through deeds; only 40% believe Jesus Christ lived a sinless life; and there are a 100 million people in America who are unchurched, the figures add up to practical atheism in America. People say they believe in God but they live like there is no God.

There are three convincing arguments to use with the skeptics. First, there is the **CAUSE-EFFECT** argument (cosmological) which says every effect must have a cause. If there is creation there must be a Creator. Charles Darwin at the end of his life said, "Disbelief crept over me at a very slow rate and at last was complete. I am like a man who has become color-blind. Though once capable of wonder, admiration and devotion in the presence of the works of God, now, not even the grandest scene could cause any such convictions and feelings to rise in my mind. For myself I do not believe that there has ever been any revelation." Given Darwin's own confession of ignorance, why is evolution still taught in our schools? The answer is that people prefer a lie to the truth. Darwin believed the cause of all creation was within the universe, in creation itself by random selection. Christians believe that all creation comes from outside the universe by an infinitely intelligent Being. Paul said in Acts 17:28 concerning God, **In whom, we live, move, and have our being**. Logically, you don't go by a house on a street, admire it, and say, "I believe that house randomly came together; there was an explosion at Lowes and suddenly all the right parts fell out of the sky coming together; with nails and without any known cause the house came into being." Only a fool would say that.

The second argument for the existence of God is the **ORDER-INTELLIGENT DESIGNER** argument (teleological). David wrote in Psalm 8, **When I consider thy heavens, the work of thy fingers, the moon and the stars, which thou hast ordained; What is man, that thou art mindful of him? and the son of man, that thou visitest him?** Look at the sun and the planets in our solar system. With perfect design and order the sun is the exact right temperature not to burn up the planets; the earth perfectly orbits the sun to set the seasons and rotates in exactly 23 hours and 56 minutes to set the days and nights. It is not random. It is set by an intelligent God. How does the human body heal itself? Is that by evolution, randomness, accident? You hope not, otherwise your body might stay randomly sick until it randomly decides to get well. If you do not believe that God exists and has created the body to heal itself, then why doesn't a car that is in an accident heal itself? The obvious answer is the car is made by man. One would readily agree there is a big difference in what man makes and what God makes.

Thirdly, there is the **REALITY-PROOF** argument (ontological). Stop and think for a moment. If God is enough of a reality in a man's mind that he denies the existence of God, that is proof the man is a fool for thinking so because if God didn't exist at all the man would not have any reason to deny His existence, would he? Another way to say it is, "Why so much effort on the part of man to deny what he doesn't believe exists in the first place." It was Rene Descartes, the French philosopher, that said, "I think, therefore I am." He was saying that his existence was proven by the presence of a thinking mind. Is the opposite then true? If he didn't have an operative mind would that mean he doesn't exist. The fact that my mind is working just a little bit is proof that I exist, am sitting where I am sitting, and am really teaching this lesson that you are reading. Or maybe I don't exist and you really are not studying this lesson. Which do you believe? In Ecclesiastes 3:11 it says God "hath set the world" (*owlam* which means eternity) in the heart of man. It is ingrained, innate, written on the conscious intuitive mind of man, that there is eternity where God dwells. The only reason a man would deny the existence of God is because he has freely chosen to ignore his logical mind. That is deliberate ignorance and spiritual suicide.

His Uniqueness

In the Ten Commandments there are two of the commandments that demand our respect of God's uniqueness: no other gods and no graven images. When Moses asked Pharaoh when he should pray for the frogs to go away in Egypt, Pharaoh cried and pleaded for immediate relief. Moses told him that he would pray and the frogs would go away so that Pharaoh would know that **there is none like unto the LORD our God (Exodus 8:10).** There is nothing worse in our lives than to let something take the place of Jehovah God in our hearts. In fact, the devout Jew recites Deuteronomy 6:4 twice a day so that he will not forget, **Hear, O Israel: The LORD our God is one LORD.** The idea of oneness here does not refer to singleness but unity. Christians believe in one God expressed in three persons: the Father, the Son, and the Holy Spirit, but all three are one God. Compare this truth to what Jesus said about a husband and a wife being "one flesh." In marriage two persons are a spiritual unity. Marriage, in the Scriptures, represents the oneness of God in his love of the church. (Ephesians 5:21-33)

Because of God's uniqueness, all the other false gods of the world are an insult to Jehovah. Idolatry is an insult to Jehovah. Polytheism is the worship of many gods, which is what the Buddhists and Hindus do. Pantheism believes that God is in all things, and that is what the American Indians followed as their worship pattern. Deism is a belief that God set it all in motion, and now takes a vacation expecting man to keep things running. This is why Islam believes so strongly it is right to kill all infidels–anyone who does not believe in Allah and Mohammed.

Christianity is the only true faith in all the world according to the Bible because of the uniqueness of Jehovah revealed in the Word of God.

His Nature

While it is indeed impossible to know all there is to know about God until we are in His presence and have perfect knowledge, there are some things we can say with surety about God's nature. Even though Romans 11:33 says His "ways are past finding out," He is not a God who doesn't want us to know Him at all. We just cannot know all there is to know of Him, because He is infinitely wise and comprehensively transcendent. Our minds cannot totally grasp God because we are human. But there are some things we know by Scripture, and these are only a small portion of the descriptive characteristics of His nature. It would be impossible to discuss them all in one lesson.

God is **spirit**. Jesus spoke of this fact to the woman at the well. The Spirit is the highest form of a being. A spirit is not limited by time or space. This is why God can be omnipresent (everywhere at all times), omnipotent (all powerful without limitations of a mortal body), and omniscient (all-knowing without the boundaries of a human intellect). Nobody controls God. Nobody can see Him in mortal flesh or they would die. Nobody can touch Him because He is not flesh, but He can touch us in spiritual ways that man cannot fully explain though evermore real.

God is **sovereign**. Paul says in Ephesians 1:11 that God "worketh all things after the counsel of his own will." The other word for sovereignty is Lordship. God, by His very nature, has the right to tell you what to do and expect your obedience. That He is totally superior over us in His character, completely amazing beyond us in His creation, and absolutely gracious in spite of us by His merciful redemption, requires nothing less than our total surrender to His Lordship.

God is **holy**. God is completely free from evil and hates sin. Habakkuk 1:13 says God's eyes are so pure He cannot even look upon evil. Four times in the Bible we read of "holy angels" (Matthew 25:31, Mark 8:38, Luke 9:26, and Revelation 14:10) But Jude 1:6 says there were angels that left their "first estate". Angels were created holy but they can lose that holiness. God can never forfeit His holiness because that is His unchanging nature, **Holy, holy, holy, is the LORD of hosts: the whole earth is full of his glory (Isaiah 6:3).** 1 Samuel 2:2 says, **There is none holy as the LORD.** God is morally perfect. This makes Him the eternal enemy of sin. His holiness is our standard of life and conduct. This is absolutely why we need a Savior. We have no capacity to live holy without His life within us.

God is **love**. Whenever a verse says, "God is something," it means He is the source and essence of that characteristic. The Bible clearly says in 1 John 4:8 that "God is love." God is the source and essence of love. That means you cannot know true love until you know God. That means you are not loving, not really loving, if you are not loving God's way–unconditionally. Men use women and women use men and call it love. It is not love. It is lust. People say God loves me just the way that I am. That is impossible if the way that you are is sinful. God cannot, will not, and must not have anything to do with sin. He came to separate the sin from the sinner. The truth is that God loves us so much that He can't leave us the way that we are. He loves us into righteousness and holiness. He does not love us if we are holy. He loves us unconditionally and turns us from unholy living.

God is **merciful and good**. The Bible says His mercies are new every morning. (Lamentations 3:23) The Bible says in Psalms 86:5, **For thou, Lord, art good, and ready to forgive; and plenteous in mercy unto all them that call upon thee.** Notice that there is a condition on God's mercy–"to all that call" upon Him. God knows the heart of every man whether that call in his heart for mercy is real or fake. Fakers forfeit God's mercy. Psalm 145:18 says, **The LORD is nigh unto all them that call upon him, to all that call upon him in truth.**

God is **truthful**. Numbers 23:19 says, **God is not a man, that he should lie; neither the son of man, that he should repent: hath he said, and shall he not do it? or hath he spoken, and shall he not make it good?** You can trust what God says no matter what circumstances seem to indicate otherwise. Jesus Christ is THE WAY, THE TRUTH, AND THE LIFE.

God is **unchanging**. This is called immutability. God is the same **yesterday, today, and forever (Hebrews 13:8).** James says there is no variableness (fickleness) or shadow of turning (shady side, something hidden) in God. This does not mean that God cannot change His actions. He just never changes His attitudes, His purposes.

God is **just**. You never have to doubt that God is fair with man. Man sometimes will doubt God's love when tragedy strikes, but man's understanding is limited. Moses said in Deuteronomy 32:4, **He is the Rock, his work is perfect: for all his ways are judgment: a God of truth and without iniquity, just and right is he.** God's holiness demands He be just. He can no more be unjust than He can be unholy. Man can be bribed, forced, perverted, and sinister. God can be none of those. It is because of God's mercy that we don't get more justice of what we deserve for our iniquity. Ezra prayed (9:13), **And after all that is come upon us for our evil deeds, and for our great trespass, seeing that thou our God hast punished us less than our iniquities deserve, and hast given us such deliverance as this.** David said, **If thou, LORD, shouldest mark iniquities, O Lord, who shall stand? But there is forgiveness with thee, that thou mayest be feared.** God never elevates one of His attributes above another. So, His love doesn't override His justice. It is His mercy that steps in the middle and gives us less than we deserve, satisfying justice through Christ's atonement and proving love through Christ's death. But, my friend, if you reject the mercies of God you will receive the full penalty of God's justice for sin no matter how much you think God loves you and will let you go free in your rebellion.

God is **great and mighty**. God has many names. His names mean something about His character. *Jehovah Jireh* means He is our Provider (Genesis 22:14). *El Shaddai* means the Almighty God (Genesis 17:1). *El Olam* means He is the Everlasting God (Genesis 21:33). God is *Adonai* which means Lord. But the word *Elohim* is used some 2,500 times in the Bible which means plentitude of might and excellence of power.

He is the One who tends to the sun in the sky as well as the sheep on the mountainside. He is the One who keeps the boundaries of the ocean in control and turns the winds loose on the mighty seas of earth. He is the One who clothes the lilies of the field and feeds every sparrow his morning breakfast. He is the One who sets Orion, Arcturus, and the Pleiades a million miles into space that they may be seen like diamonds on a black velvet sky at night. But isn't it more amazing that He will be a Father to you and me? **For ye have not received the spirit of bondage again to fear; but ye have received the Spirit of adoption, whereby we cry, Abba, Father (Romans 8:15).** The tender affection of Jehovah is unmatched and deserves our utmost adoration, service and love.

Reflection Station:

1. How would you seek to argue for the existence of God to someone who doesn't believe God exists?

2. Can you match the following numbers (explanations for God's existence) with the correct letters (scientific name)?

   1   Since every effect must have a cause, then creation must have a Creator.

   2   The incredible order and intelligent design of the universe demands belief in an Intelligent Designer, God Himself.

   3   If man has enough conscience and logical mind to reject God's existence it must mean that God exists. Why put up such a fuss to refuse to believe in something that you don't believe in anyway.

   A   Teleological Argument

   B   Ontological Argument

   C   Cosmological Argument

3. What is the Hebrew name for God that indicates He is Great and Mighty?

LESSON TWO
Doctrine of Christ

LESSON TITLE: The Doctrine of Christ - Theology

SCRIPTURE: Galatians 1:6-8, 1 Timothy 2:5, Hebrews 3:1

TRUTH TO GAIN: Only the right Jesus can save your soul.

The Importance of Accurate Doctrine

Galatians 1:6-8 tells us that there is a curse upon anyone who preaches the wrong Christ and the wrong gospel. Not only did Paul warn against teachers of false doctrine, so did the Apostle John. 2 John 7 says, **For many deceivers are entered into the world, who confess not that Jesus Christ is come in the flesh. This is a deceiver and an antichrist.** Whoever does not believe and teach the right Christ is an antichrist.

In the 1980's, Robert Funk started what is called The Jesus Seminar. In that seminar, which has gone all over the world, Funk taught that we should "give Jesus a demotion...it is no longer credible to think of Jesus as divine." That makes Robert Funk an antichrist.

Jehovah's Witnesses teach that Jesus Christ was Michael the Archangel before he came to earth. According to them, Jesus the person became the Messiah at his baptism which makes him "a god" but not the God, mighty but not Almighty. Jehovah's Witnesses are antichrists.

Mormons teach that God had sex with Mary and that is how Jesus Christ was born. According to Mormonism, Jesus Christ is the spirit brother of Lucifer. This is blasphemous and Mormons are antichrists.

Where do people get these kind of doctrines? The answer is in 1 Timothy 4:1, **Now the Spirit speaketh expressly, that in the latter times some shall depart from the faith, giving heed to seducing spirits, and doctrines of devils**. The liar of hell seeks to malign the character of the

Biblical Jesus and sends his demons to sow the seeds of falsehood in the foolish minds of men.

His Eternal Preexistence

Jesus Christ, contrary to most teaching of cults and false religionists, did not all of a sudden come into being at the time of the New Testament. Jesus Christ was and is eternally God before time and earth ever existed. There are many evidences to that fact. In the very first chapter of the first book of the Bible you read these words, **And God said, Let us make man in our image (Genesis 1:26).** Why doesn't that verse have God saying, "let **ME** make man in **MY** image?" Because there is more than one person in the Godhead present in that verse. Christians believe in the doctrine of the Trinity, that God is one God expressed in three persons, all coequal, and perfectly divine–God the Father, God the Son, and God the Holy Spirit. All three were there in the beginning. You read of God creating the heaven and the earth in verse one. You read of the Spirit moving upon the face of the waters in verse two. But where is Jesus? He is most certainly there though you may miss Him if your eyes cannot discern His presence. When you find the word "God" in Genesis 1, it is the Hebrew word *Elohim*. All Hebrew words with "im" on the end of the word is a plural word. *El* is God. *Elohim* is the Godhead. All three persons of the Godhead are wrapped up in that word.

Jesus Christ is in Genesis 1 as the Creator. That fact is confirmed by Paul in Colossians 1:16,

> **For by him (Christ) were all things created, that are in heaven, and that are in earth, visible and invisible, whether they be thrones, or dominions, or principalities, or powers: all things were created by him, and for him.**

The stars were made for Him to give him glory. The universe was made for Him to give Him glory. If you were going to try and visit the closest star in our galaxy you would have to get aboard a jet that could travel 600 miles per hour and it would take you four and a half million years to arrive there. There are a 100 billion other stars in our galaxy, the Milky Way, which would take you trillions of years to reach. Then beyond our

Milky Way galaxy the astronomers say we have another 100 billion galaxies. The universe was made by Him and for Him to give Him the glory He deserves.

Those scientists that sit behind the big telescopes are telling us now that the universe and the galaxies seem to be expanding. That is not surprising when you read Isaiah 40:22,

> **It is he that sitteth upon the circle of the earth, and the inhabitants thereof are as grasshoppers; that stretcheth out the heavens as a curtain, and spreadeth them out as a tent to dwell in.**

Jesus did all that as Creator and He did it for Himself. But we need to be reminded that if all things were created by Him and for Him, hell was created that way too (Matthew 25:41). Jesus created Hell to glorify Himself. That sounds strange doesn't it? But hell is the place created by Christ to punish sin. Hell will reveal the righteousness, wrath, justice and holiness of Jesus Christ. The wrath of God against sin glorifies Jesus just as much as the love, grace and mercy of God. If that were not so we would have to live in heaven with murderers, rapists, homosexuals, liars, and thieves.

Jesus Christ is in Genesis 1 as Redeemer. In John 8:58 Jesus said, **Verily, verily, I say unto you, Before Abraham was, I am.** Now, that statement was the most hated statement of all of Jesus' ministry. All Jews, thinking they were the sons of Abraham, by following the laws of Moses and circumcision felt they were in God's kingdom. Jesus told them He was before Abraham and you don't get into heaven by bloodlines but by bloodshed. In Jesus Christ's High Priestly prayer of John 17:5 He prayed, **And now, O Father, glorify thou me with thine own self with the glory which I had with thee before the world was.** Christ was here before ever a man existed, and had glory with the Father. He is called the Everlasting Father in Isaiah 9:6. He is called the Ancient of Days in Daniel 7. But most significantly in Revelation 13:8 He is the **lamb slain BEFORE the foundation of the world.** Calvary and salvation was no afterthought of God. In the infinite knowledge of God He knew man would fall in sin before he was ever made in the likeness and image of God. So, you could rightly say that God had things fixed before they were ever broken. Christ was there before there ever was a thing called sin. Christ was the Lamb of God in the beginning before there was a beginning to earth, just as much as He was the mighty second Person of the Trinity in Creation.

His Virgin Birth

The true Christ was virgin born. Herbert Lockyer wrote,

> By the virgin birth we are to understand that, contrary to the course of nature, Jesus was divinely conceived in the womb of Mary, the Holy Spirit becoming the love knot between our Lord's two natures. In such a conception, deity and humanity were fused together and Jesus came forth as the God-man.

Genesis 3:15 predicted this birth 4000 years ahead of time by saying it would occur by the "seed of a woman." The Hebrews never said that about someone's genealogy. It was always referred to as coming from the man's seed. In fact, the Bible writers guarded their words when they described the birth of Jesus. Luke 1 will talk of Elizabeth "bearing" Zecharias, a son, but in the same chapter it says that a son will be "born" of Mary. He makes sure the readers know the perplexity of Mary's mind when she questions such a possibility, since she testified "I know not a man."

In the genealogy of Matthew 1 Jacob BEGAT Joseph but later he says, "Mary of whom was BORN Jesus." Jesus was not begotten of man, but was the only begotten Son of God. The Apostle Paul is careful with his words also. Comparing to Matthew, who says John the Baptist was born (*gennao* in the Greek: Matthew 11:11), Paul speaks of Christ in Galatians 4:4 as being "made" (*gennetos* in the Greek) of a woman. The latter, *gennetos*, has the meaning "to generate, cause to be, come into being." Christ had a supernatural conception, not a supernatural birth. Mary had to have Jesus the same way women today birth their babies, but she didn't have a hospital.

The virgin birth of Jesus Christ is absolutely essential in our beliefs, a cardinal doctrine of the faith, without which we would have no Savior.

If He was not virgin born He could not have been fully divine and without sin. The sin of Adam passed to all men born of natural conception between a man and a woman.

Now what are the possibilities of this miraculous birth of Christ? Well besides the fact that He was virgin born, which no other child in all of history has ever been born that way, Jesus was also of the seed of Abraham, of the tribe of Judah, of the branch of David, and born in the remote Judean village of Bethlehem. Here is the probability of that happening. The reason Jesus was of the seed of Abraham was that He would fulfill the Abrahamic covenant, **In thee shall all the families of the earth be blessed (Genesis 12:3).** Jesus Christ appeared in human flesh forty-two generations removed from Abraham according to Matthew 1:17. Many families have been wiped out in just ten generations with no offspring to carry on the line. Jesus Christ could have well been an Hittite, a Perizzite, a Jebusite, a Girgashite, an Amorite, or some other "Whatchamacall-ite." But no, the prophecy was fulfilled and it would be a conservative estimate to say the chance He would fall under the genealogy of Abraham would be one chance in a hundred.

Take that and add it to the fact he was of the tribe of Judah, you will then multiply 12 times 100, since there were twelve tribes in Israel and you get a probability of 1 chance in 1200 that Christ would come of this one tribe. Mormons blatantly lie against Scripture when they say Jesus was of the tribe of Benjamin because Jerusalem belonged to the Benjamite. Since He was not of the tribe of Benjamin, the fact that Christ came of the line of David (Judah) is also incredible. David's father Jesse had eight sons which increases the improbability of the prophetic descent by 1 chance in 9600. David's father Jesse would have never existed if Boaz had not taken Ruth to wife and became David's great grandfather. That would make a conservative estimate of one chance in a thousand that a Jewish man would marry a widowed Moabite. Now we are up to one chance in 9,600,000. Add the virgin birth and the city of His birth among thousands in Judah and you have a probability of one chance in over 9.6 trillion. The odds of prophecy being fulfilled promotes the accuracy of the Word of God and the Sovereign control of God. What does that mean to you when you know that Christ did all of this to come for you?

His Sinless Life

The greatest verse in all the Bible on the sinlessness of Jesus Christ is without doubt 2 Corinthians 5:21, **For he hath made him to be sin for us, who knew no sin; that we might be made the righteousness of God in him.** The word *know* in that text is the word for "experiential knowledge," not just intellectual knowledge. Jesus knew about sin intellectually, of course, but he never participated, had any connection with, nor ever could testify of experience in sin. He expressed that to the Pharisees one day, **Which of you convinceth me of sin? And if I say the truth, why do ye not believe me?" (John 8:46).** They could not pin a sin, not one, on Jesus. They had no reason to rebuke him, correct him, or fault him. Paul said, **He was in all points tempted like as we are, yet without sin (Hebrews 4:15).** He not only had a virgin birth but also a virgin life. If Jesus Christ was not totally sinless He could not be our redeemer.

Many movies in our day have Jesus so human He cannot appear divine the way they portray him. Martin Scorcese in 1988 directed the film *The Last Temptation of Christ* where he portrayed Christ as having lustful thoughts on the cross, engaging in sexual encounters in his mind. It brought outrage from Christians. The movie world nominated Scorcese for an academy award for such blasphemy. In 2006 Dopie Opie, Ron Howard, directed *The Davinci Code*, a movie based upon Ron Brown's fictional book, and actually claims the Holy Grail was a code word for Mary Magdalene, the wife of Christ, which went missing because the disciples could not follow a woman after Jesus was gone. Despite church boycots, and sidewalk protests, this movie grossed over $80 million making it the second most lucrative film of this era.

Fierce debates have arisen on the subject of whether it was possible for Jesus Christ to sin. Did His deity prevent the possibility of sinning? Did His humanity open up the same temptations to Christ as every man faces? The Hebrews 4:15 passage and the 2 Corinthians 5:21 passage answers that question definitively. It would be wrong to say that Christ could not sin. It would be perfectly right to say that Christ would not sin, ever. He was so fully human that He could be touched and feel our infirmities (weaknesses). There is no temptation that has ever come to you or me that He did not face when Satan tempted Him in the wilderness. If Jesus

Christ could not be tempted to sin, then that whole scene in the wilderness is a hoax, a meaningless display. However, Christ was so fully divine that the words of John 14:30 strike a clearer note, **For the prince of this world cometh, and hath nothing in me.** He felt it all, faced it all, and resisted it all. Only one who could be tempted with sin, yet remain without sin, could atone for sin.

His Vicarious, Substitionary Death

If those words in Isaiah 53:3-5 do not come to haunt the sinner with enormous guilt for what our sin put Jesus Christ through to save us, we're the most brazen, calloused, hardhearted creatures in all the world.

> **He is despised and rejected of men; a man of sorrows, and acquainted with grief: and we hid as it were our faces from him; he was despised, and we esteemed him not. Surely he hath borne our griefs, and carried our sorrows: yet we did esteem him stricken, smitten of God, and afflicted. But he was wounded for our transgressions, he was bruised for our iniquities: the chastisement of our peace was upon him; and with his stripes we are healed.**

The word vicarious has a similar meaning to substitionary, but it goes one step further. The person who is the substitute sympathetically experiences what the real victim faces. Jesus Christ came in full sympathy to our death sentence for sin. He was willing to take our place on the cross.

The death of Christ is mentioned 175 times in the gospels. One-third of Matthew, one-third of Mark, one-fourth of Luke, and one-half of John is devoted to the account of Jesus' death. Mark 10:45 says that Jesus gave his life a "ransom for many." The word for ransom is the first Greek word learned by new students to Greek, **lutron** from the root *luo*. It means "to loosen." The atoning work of Christ's death on the cross set us free, loosened us from a sure death bondage to the cursed work of sin. The death of Christ not only released us from a curse, it reconciled us back to God. Paul records the fact, **To wit, that God was in Christ, reconciling the world unto himself, not imputing their trespasses unto them; and hath committed unto us the word of reconciliation (2 Corinthians**

5:19). By sin we were enemies to God. By blood we have been made sons, fellow heirs, friends, and temples of the Holy Spirit. By our attitudes and our actions we rarely exhibit the deserved appreciation for the death price Christ paid to release us from condemnation.

There are some interesting facts about Jesus' death that no other man can claim. He predicted His manner of death before it ever happened (Matthew 17:22-23). He claimed His death would keep the whole world from perishing if they would believe on Him (John 3:16). Jesus claimed that His death would defeat Satan (John 12:31). His death was voluntary, not forced. He gave His life, no man took it (John 10:18). He was buried in a borrowed tomb of a rich man, Joseph of Arimathea, but Isaiah knew that 750 years before Christ was ever born (Isaiah 53:9). Salvation is POSSIBLE through Christ's death on the cross, but it is only ACTUAL by our belief in Christ's death, burial and resurrection.

His Resurrection and Ascension

The Bible says in 1 Corinthians 15, **For I delivered unto you first of all that which I also received, how that Christ died for our sins according to the scriptures; And that he was buried, and that he rose again the third day according to the scriptures.** The completion of Christ's saving work is His resurrection and ascension. This is why Romans 4:25 says, **Who was delivered for our offences, and was raised again for our justification.** Do you know why the death of Christ alone was not sufficient to promise us heaven? All our sins, all our offences were taken care of in Christ's death on the cross. Wouldn't that be enough? No, Jesus had to be raised out of the tomb to prove that God accepted that sacrifice to justify us in the eyes of the Father and bring peace to the wrathful state between sinner and God. There was enmity. There was broken fellowship. It was repaired at Calvary and registered at the garden tomb that was empty on that third day. The resurrection was God's receipt for Calvary.

What proof do we have of the resurrection? Are 514 witnesses enough proof? If only one person had seen Him after His entombment there might be cause to doubt the story, but 514 people cannot be wrong (See (1 Corinthians 15:5-8). What does the resurrection mean for us today? It means that Christ has triumphed over the last enemy of man–death (1

Corinthians 15:26). This is why you need Him unless you think you can defeat death all by yourself. The resurrection means that we can go out in resurrection power to share the gospel of Christ around the world. The resurrection means that since Christ was the firstfruits of resurrection we have the promise of a raised and glorified body. Now, what guarantees that final resurrection of the dead is the occupation Jesus took at the point of His ascension. Hebrews 7:25 says, **Wherefore he is able also to save them to the uttermost that come unto God by him, seeing he ever liveth to make intercession for them.** Jesus ascended into Heaven to guarantee our advance reservations. He is the Eternal Desk Clerk making sure when you get there your room is ready.

His Return

The Bible promises a second coming of Jesus Christ to this earth. It will be the same Jesus that came the first time. The angel from the ascension point of the Mount of Olives said, **This same Jesus, which is taken up from you into heaven, shall so come in like manner as ye have seen him go into heaven.** It won't be the Jehovah Witnesses' Jesus. It won't be the Mormon's Jesus. It won't be the Mohammedan's Jesus. It won't be the Hollywood Jesus. It will be *Yeshua Hamashiach*, which is Hebrew for Jesus, the Anointed Messiah, the son of Jehovah God. Belief in any other Jesus is sure condemnation to the soul.

Reflection Station:

1. Give a definition of the Doctrine of the Trinity and explain how you know that all three Persons of the Godhead were involved in the Genesis creation.

2. How important is the virgin birth of Jesus Christ to the power of our salvation?

3. Which of the following are true statements?

    A. Jesus predicted the manner of his death before it happened.

    B. Jesus claimed His death would keep the whole world from perishing in their sin if they would believe on Him.

    C. Jesus claimed His death would defeat Satan.

    D. Jesus claimed His death was voluntary not forced.

    E. Isaiah predicted that Jesus would be buried in a rich man's tomb.

4. If Jesus Christ had died on the cross but was never raised from the dead, could we be saved? (See Romans 4:25)

LESSON THREE
Doctrine of the Holy Spirit

LESSON TITLE: The Doctrine of the Holy Spirit - Pneumatology

SCRIPTURE: John 14:26, John 15:26, John 16:7-14

TRUTH TO GAIN: The Holy Spirit plays a major role in the life of the believer, and, therefore, it behooves us to take full advantage of His ministry in our lives.

A Barrel of Controversy

No other doctrine of the faith perhaps has had more controversy surrounding it than the Doctrine of the Holy Spirit. It wasn't until the 3rd century A.D. that a man by the name of Tertullian began to write a thorough doctrine of the Holy Spirit to clear up some of the controversy. In A.D. 157-171 there were a group of people called the Montanists, followers of the teacher Montanus. The Montanists taught and believed that the Holy Spirit was giving new revelations by the Holy Spirit and there were a group of "new prophets" that arose. This was the forerunner of the modern day Pentecostal movement. There really isn't anything new under the sun.

In A.D. 200 a man by the name of Sabellius arose and began to teach that God was one God who wore three masks, one for the father, one for the son, and one for the Holy Spirit. This made God a schizophrenic who deceived people. Tertullian fought this heresy about the Trinity of God. Tertullian was the first man to coin the term "trinity," and he taught that God was one God with expression of three persons. Sabellius taught that the Holy Spirit was just an influence of God through a mask called the Holy Spirit.

Then in the fourth century a man named Arius raised another heresy about the Holy Spirit. Arius taught that God was only a Father who created the Son and the Holy Spirit. The other two persons, the Son and the Holy Spirit, were not coequal with God and were only impersonal forces that God used to get His business done. In 381 A.D. the Council of Constantinople corrected this false doctrine by adding words to the Nicene Creed saying, "And I believe in the Holy Ghost, the Lord, and Giver of Life, who proceedeth from the Father and the Son; who with the Father and the Son together is worshiped and glorified; who spake by the Prophets."

The Jehovah's Witnesses say that the Holy Spirit is nothing more than a force (Reasoning from the Scriptures, 1985, pp. 406-407). The Church of Christ says concerning Acts 2:38, "Then Peter said unto them, Repent, and be baptized every one of you in the name of Jesus Christ for the remission of sins, and ye shall receive the gift of the Holy Ghost," that "The construction of the English sentence does not necessarily imply that if one receives remission of sins, that therefore one MUST receive the gift of the Holy Spirit as well...the forgiveness of sins is ongoing forever; you can get that by repenting and being baptized; however, the additional gift has expired and no longer comes with the original product" (Berryville, Arkansas Church of Christ). Then the Pentecostals tell us that the Holy Spirit is an additional gift after you get saved, a second experience beyond your salvation where you will get the "baptism of the Holy Ghost," and you will speak in tongues. What is a person supposed to believe about the Holy Spirit? Believe the Bible! Believe nothing but the Bible! Do not believe those who have twisted the Bible!

Before Creation

To begin with the right understanding about the Holy Spirit we must go back to Genesis. Genesis 1:2 says, **The Spirit of God moved upon the face of the waters.** This is a direct reference to the Holy Spirit. How do we know that? Because God is spirit and if this was referring to the first person of the trinity all the biblical writer had to do was say, "God moved upon the face of the waters." But He says "the Spirit **of** God," and that word *of* is very important. The Spirit of God is referring to the third person of the Trinity.

Now, the question is if the third person of the Trinity is just a force, or an influence, or a part of God's creation. We know that the Spirit of God is not a part of God's creation because in Genesis 1:2 He is taking part in the Genesis or the beginning of creation. There are several Scriptures in the Bible to prove the Spirit of God is a person of the Godhead, not just an impersonal force or influence. In Acts 13:2 the Holy Spirit speaks. Forces do not speak. In Ephesians 4:30 the Holy Spirit can be grieved. You can only do that to a person. In 1 Corinthians 12:11 you discover that the Holy Spirit gives out spiritual gifts according to his will. He has a will, a conscious ability to make decisions. Forces and influences cannot do that. Water is a force but it cannot decide on its own where to flow. That is governed by the laws of gravity and resistance set up by God himself. Electricity is a force or influence but thankfully it doesn't have a will of its own. Electrons flow in a manner prescribed by the Creator. Romans 8:26-27 says the Spirit groans and makes intercessions for us through His mind. Forces can't groan and they don't have a mind.

It is also important to note that the Holy Spirit is always referred to by personal pronouns in the masculine gender. This is a bit strange however because the word for Spirit is *pneuma*, which is in the neuter gender. Even in the English language we say "he," referring to a male, and "she," referring to a female and "it," referring to neither male nor female. *It* is the neuter gender, but with *pneuma* there is always a masculine pronoun or masculine verb in the Greek language. This is so that we will know that the Holy Spirit is not a "she" and is not a "force."

Crucial for Salvation

We are told in the Scriptures that without the aid of the Holy Spirit no man can be saved. The Holy Spirit is involved in seven ways to the work of saving a soul. First of all, He is the one who **convicts of the need of salvation**. John 16:8 says, **And when he is come, he will reprove the world of sin, and of righteousness, and of judgment.** Without the conviction of sin a person cannot get saved. The mind must be illumined from the darkness of sin that clouds the understanding of man in his cursed condition. 2 Corinthians 4:3-4 says, **But if our gospel be hid, it is hid to them that are lost: In whom the god of this world hath blinded the minds of them which believe not, lest the light of the glorious gospel of Christ, who is the image of God, should shine unto them.** It is the Holy Spirit that turns back that blindness and lets the light of the gospel shine in.

Secondly, the Holy Spirit **draws the soul to God for salvation**. John

6:44 says, **No man can come to me, except the Father which hath sent me draw him: and I will raise him up at the last day.** The Father does that drawing through the Holy Spirit. The gentle wooing of the Holy Spirit to Christ is in the form of conviction and urging us to repent of sin and be saved.

After the conviction of sin and drawing of the Spirit upon our repentance and belief in Christ, the Holy Spirit **performs the transaction of the salvation experience.** There is the quickening from spiritual death to spiritual life. Colossians 2:13 says, **And you, being dead in your sins and the uncircumcision of your flesh, hath he quickened together with him, having forgiven you all trespasses.** Since salvation is being "in Christ," then salvation happens supernaturally in the same manner that Christ bought our salvation–through the price of death and the trust of resurrection. As sinners we are dead in trespasses and sin (Ephesians 2:1). To come back to life we have to be quickened (re-given life). How did that happen for Christ? Romans 8:11 says, **But if the Spirit of him that raised up Jesus from the dead dwell in you, he that raised up Christ from the dead shall also quicken your mortal bodies by his Spirit that dwelleth in you.** At the moment of salvation, according to 1 Corinthians 12:13, the Spirit of God baptizes you spiritually, invisibly, and legally into the body or family of Christ. You become a member of Christ's family. That is the "baptism of the Holy Spirit." It is not being baptized "with" the Spirit but being baptized "by" the Spirit into the spiritual body of Christ. It is a union with the Lord and His Church. So we are quickened by the Spirit, and then the Spirit of God indwells us. Jesus told His disciples one day that the Spirit of God had been with them but would be "in them" (John 14:17). Since Pentecost the promise of the coming Holy Spirit is for indwelling. This is really crucial for salvation because Romans 8:9 says if you have not the Spirit of Christ dwelling in you, you are not saved, you don't belong to Christ, you are lost, and you won't make it to heaven.

Fourthly, the Holy Spirit of God is the **operator in the renewing of salvation.** Titus 3:5 says, **Not by works of righteousness which we have done, but according to his mercy he saved us, by the washing of regeneration, and renewing of the Holy Ghost.** There are a lot of people who claimed to be Christians but there hasn't been much renewing. The Bible says in 2 Corinthians 5:17 that to be in Christ "old things are passed away; behold, all things are become new." To understand this change you have to know the Bible language of the passage and what it says. Two things happen: 1) old things are passed away and this is an aorist tense of the verb which means at a point in time, once and for all, the old is permanently passed away; 2) all things are become new which is a perfect active indicative tense meaning it stays that way, a permanent state of being new. If you don't have those two things you don't have a person that is *in Christ*. If a person goes through the motions of a conversion experience but turns back out into sin as an enjoyable practice of their life, they have mocked God, mocked salvation, and mocked the Holy Spirit. There is no renewal. There is no operation of the Holy Spirit. There is no salvation. They can believe anything they want to believe, but if it doesn't happen according to the Word of God it did not happen. There will be a lot of people who will die believing they were saved but they didn't change.

Fifthly, the Spirit of God is responsible for **guaranteeing our salvation**. Your good works are not your guarantee of salvation. Your going to church doesn't guarantee your salvation. Salvation is by grace and the keeping of your salvation is also by grace. It is the grace of God that He would ever consider coming to live inside your being through the presence of the Holy Spirit. The indwelling Holy Spirit is your only witness you'll finally make it to heaven.

This is why the sin of the blasphemy of the Holy Ghost is such a soul-damning sin. When a person becomes so anti-Christian, so belligerent against the message of Christ, so hardened in his/her heart against getting saved, which is the cutting edge of the Holy Spirit's work, and that person blasphemes (malign or criticize with an evil heart) the Holy Spirit, this marks the boundary and the crossing of that which the Holy Spirit decides He will not ever live in that person's soul. It is the unpardonable sin. It places the permanent signpost upon the heart of that unbeliever "a condemned dwelling." This is also the reason why Ephesians 4:30 says, **And grieve not the holy Spirit of God, whereby ye are sealed unto the day of redemption.**

Does this in any way mean you can grieve the Spirit and lose your salvation? Never! The Bible never says that! But you can grieve the Spirit and lose His testimony in your heart that you are truly saved and safe from a devil's hell. The worst thing ever for a human soul is to go to hell, separated from God. The second worst thing in your life is to be on your way to heaven and not ever able to know it because the witness of the Spirit in your soul has been shut down and remains silent.

The Holy Spirit, sixthly, is responsible for the **assurance of salvation**. Read it again. Romans 8:16 says, **The Spirit itself beareth witness with our spirit, that we are the children of God.** Also 1 John 4:13 says, **Hereby know we that we dwell in him, and he in us, because he hath given us of his Spirit.** I like 1 John 5:13 but I also like 1 John 4:13 even better. Why? Because plenty of people have good assurance of salvation at the time of salvation, but a lot of them lose that assurance after the time of salvation. What good is it to receive a wedding band on your wedding day and to subsequently lose it in your house and never be able to find it as long as you live? That is a very distressing prospect. Christians don't lose the Spirit of God but they can lose the assurance ministry of the Spirit of God. 2 Corinthians 1:22 says, **Who hath also sealed us, and given the earnest of the Spirit in our hearts.** (See also 2 Corinthians 5:5, Ephesians 1:13-14) Ephesians 1:13-14 says the Spirit of God is the **earnest of our inheritance until the redemption of the purchased possession, unto the praise of his glory.** That word *earnest* is a Hebrew word in the New Testament which means a part of the purchase money given in advance to guarantee the possession of what is purchased. Now, there you have one of two guarantees of eternal security for the believer. One part is here in your heart. One part is there in heaven by Christ's protection. The Holy Spirit guarantees your place in heaven.

According to 1 Peter 1:4 Christ, by the virtue of His resurrection power, reserves your place in heaven. Have you ever lost an important receipt in your filing system? You know you purchased the item. You want to exchange it for something better. But you can't find that receipt. You know how perplexing that is? This is why a Christian must not grieve the Spirit because He is the receipt for our inheritance in heaven. We can shove Him in the back closet of our pile of carnal pursuits in life to the point that we have let Him go missing and we no longer sense His assurance of our salvation. That is an awful place to be in spiritually.

Finally, the Holy Spirit is in charge of **"working out our salvation."** Philippians 2:12-13 says, **Wherefore, my beloved, as ye have always**

obeyed, not as in my presence only, but now much more in my absence, work out your own salvation with fear and trembling. For it is God which worketh in you both to will and to do of his good pleasure. This is not working to be saved. It is working because we are saved. This working is done within you. Who is the person of the Godhead that dwells within you? The Holy Spirit works from within for several things to glorify God and Jesus. He produces fruit (Galatians 5:22-23). He calls and commissions pastors (Acts 20:28). He empowers for witnessing (Luke 24:49). He will give you victory over the pull and temptations of your flesh (Romans 8:2-4). He is your teacher and guide in the truth of the Word of God (John 16:13). He gives the believer spiritual gifts to use for God's glory to build up the Church (1 Corinthians 12:4-11). He fills the believer by controlling his/her thoughts, attitudes and actions for the glory of God (Ephesians 5:18) This is only touching the hem of the garment in His ministry through believers.

What About Speaking in Tongues

This is the question that most people are concerned about when the ministry of the Holy Spirit is discussed. Isn't that a shame? With all the other things to discover, deliberate, and dive into concerning the Holy Spirit and the major subject of interest becomes tongues. That reality obviously demonstrates the shallow faith and maturity of Christians who do that. But we will answer the questions.

Believers are baptized by the Spirit once at salvation (1 Corinthians 12:13). There is no such thing as the Baptism of the Holy Ghost as the Pentecostals teach it. There is daily filling of the Holy Spirit which controls the believer, not a turning loose of that believer to be a spectacle (Ephesians 5:18, notice that passage says nothing about tongues). Paul downplayed tongue speaking as unintelligible, harmful, immature, and the source of controversy in the Corinthian church (1 Corinthians 14:2, 16, 20, 33). In the book of Acts tongue speaking is *glossa* in Greek and means a language. The miracle at Pentecost was the miracle of hearing not the miracle of speaking. (Acts 2:6 proving it was a language).

Is there such a thing as a prayer language that is ecstatic gibberish which a person can pray in tongues and not have to understand? Some think so according to 1 Corinthians 14:13-19. But if you do it you cannot do it in the church without interpretation. A heavenly prayer language is without understanding and declared by Paul to be unedifying, barren and unfruitful. It has absolutely nothing to offer to the church. There are some 264 references to the Holy Spirit in the New Testament–three times the number in the Old Testament. The Holy Spirit is mentioned in 24 of the New Testament books. There are eight writers of the New Testament–and all eight make mention of the Holy Spirit. You would think that with all of that people could get the doctrine straight.

Reflection Station:

1.   What is the official name for the study of the Doctrine of the Holy Spirit?

2.   Why is there so much controversy about the ministry of the Holy Spirit? Could it be that Satan, since he has been kicked out of heaven, would like to confuse people about the doctrine of salvation (Pentecostals teach that there is a second experience of grace which is called the Baptism of the Holy Spirit) which is crucial to our ability to go to heaven? See Romans 8:9,15 and 1 Timothy 4:1

3.   Is it possible that there is pride associated with the so-called "Baptism of the Holy Ghost"? (See Romans 12:3)

4.   Can you find one mention of the boasted experience of being "slain in the Spirit" within the pages of God's Word? The Apostle Paul's conversion experience on the Damascus Road is not at all fitting to this claim.

LESSON FOUR
Doctrine of Satan

LESSON TITLE: The Doctrine of Satan - Demonology (from *daimonion* translated devil in N.T. The other word is *diabolos* which means the devil.)

SCRIPTURE: Ezekiel 28:11-19, Isaiah 14:12-15

TRUTH TO GAIN: Satan is a real, personal foe to the Christian who must be discerned and resisted in the power of Christ, Calvary, and through the Holy Spirit.

Where the Devil Did the Devil Come From?

You cannot see him but nevertheless he is very present and a sinister destroyer. He is called by Paul in Ephesians 2:2, **the prince of the power of the air, the spirit that now worketh in the children of disobedience.** He is as close as the very air we breathe. He is a prince which means he is a ruler, and if we let him he can rule our hearts, control us, deceive us, blind us, and use us for evil. He is behind the finger that pulls the trigger of the murderer's gun. He is operating the butcher's scalpel posing as a doctor doing the dastardly deed of abortion. He is the manager of the tongue on the witness stand telling lies because he is the Father of lies. He is the embodied spirit of the bartender, liquor store clerk, and waitress who serves the intoxicating brew of hell, be it in a bottle with the true poison label right on the front or served in a fancy, glistening goblet on the finest restaurant table.

But lest you think he is the mastermind of only the filthiest of deeds, you must know that he is behind every backstabbing and slandering remark between Christians who faithfully go to church. He is the cook who stirs the pot of vengeance between those who have experienced the love and mercy of Christ but give in to their flesh to be unforgiving. He is the director of the drama of jealousy. He is the schemer at the drawing board of greed. He is the salesman at the auction mart of lust. He is totally responsible for the "way that seemeth right unto man," but hides the fine print of the death clause at the bottom. He has many names: Beelzebub, the Dragon, the Serpent, the accuser of the brethren, the prince of this world, the god of this world, the roaring lion, the wicked one, the Adversary, and Belial, but all his aliases simply reveal his diabolical purposes in seeking to destroy the works of God.

It would be wrong to say that the devil came from God, even though he is a created being. God never created anything evil. But God's creation can turn evil. The cherub named Lucifer made himself the devil. Isaiah 14:12 is the only time his original name appears in Scripture. Literally in Hebrew *Lucifer* means "the bright one." The bright one became the prince of darkness. Ezekiel 28:14 calls him the "anointed cherub that covereth." That reference gives us two disturbing facts about his original being. He was a cherub, one of the top four ranks of heavenly beings created by God. There are cherubim, seraphim, archangels, and regular angels. Popular depictions of angels show them with wings, but the scriptures only assume that regular angels have wings, though it never directly says so. Revelation speaks of them flying (Revelation 14:6; 19:17) but we cannot prove that the lowest order of angels have wings, only the ability to fly. But cherubim have two sets of wings and seraphim have three sets of wings (see Isaiah 6:2, Ezekiel 1:1-28 and Ezekiel 10:15,20 which identifies these four living creatures as cherubim). Lucifer with his four wings covered the throne of God. That meant he guarded the throne to protect and defend it. The very thing he was created to do, he violated with pride.

When was Satan created? It is a fair assumption to say that Satan was created when all the angels were created. On which of the six days of creation were these angels made? Some scholars believe that Lucifer was created before day one. There is a teaching that since Genesis 1:1 says God created the heavens and the earth, and the very next verse says it was "without form and void," that God could not have created something imperfect, without form and void, chaotic and empty as some would translate it. Have you ever butted into a conversation when somebody wasn't finished what they were saying, and you misunderstood completely what they were trying to say? Such as a husband who says, "Last Friday I had all I could take and I beat my wife..." You are shocked and question the spousal abuse and they finish their statement: "Last Friday I had all I could take in my car, and I beat my wife to the Dairy

Queen." The phrase "without form and void" does not in any way suggest the wild, fictitious, interpretation that Lucifer rebelled in the time between the first two verses of Genesis causing God to cast him out to the earth. To accept that interpretation is an acknowledgment of a desolate, chaotic earth which was the result of Satan's fall. It accepts a perfect earth until his judgment.

No, we believe that Lucifer had to have been created some time before day six when man was created because it was Satan who tempted Eve and Adam in the garden. We also believe that God must have created the angels before day four of creation because of what Scripture says in Job 38:6,7. **Whereupon are the foundations thereof fastened? or who laid the corner stone thereof; When the morning stars sang together, and all the sons of God shouted for joy?**

Five times in the Old Testament there is a reference to the "sons of God," and in all five occasions it is a reference to angels. In fact, Job 2:1 says these sons of God and also Satan presented themselves before God to argue the case of Job. The question then becomes "what are the foundations of the earth and the corner stone that was laid?" This possibly is a reference to the gravitational forces of the earth in relation to the size, distance, and position of the sun, moon, and stars. God created all of this, set it up just right as the foundations and corner stone upon which the earth is stabilized. The earth will not fall apart with tidal waves should the moon be too close. The earth would not be uninhabitable with molten heat like Mars had the sun been a bit larger. The "foundations" includes the gravitational pull of the moon which keeps us from leaning too far towards Jupiter's gravitational pull, which in turn would cause an ice age or greenhouse effect unsuitable for habitation by man on this planet. The angels could have witnessed all this in the creation of Day Four and sung for joy.

The Rebellion and Fall of Satan

Lucifer had a high position, a noble calling to guard the throne of God, but he rebelled in pride and lost his privileged position. He has not been cast out of heaven yet, contrary to what some believe. That does not happen till Revelation 12:7-9, where there will be war in heaven just prior to the setting up of Christ's Kingdom on the earth. Twice in Job (1:7, 2:2) it says that Satan goes "to and fro in the earth,...walking up and down in it." According to Ephesians 2:2 he is the prince of the power of the air. According to 1 Peter 5:8 he is a "roaring lion" who walketh about, which means he moves right on this earth. His territory of influence is vast and his power is enormous. Christians err on two sides concerning Satan's power. Some don't even want to talk about Satan, whereas some boast that he is a defeated foe. The Pentecostal-leaning saints brag about their personal victory over the devil. Others put down those who battle with the archenemy of God and man saying they give the devil too much credit.

The conflicting views and approaches to dealing with Satan are so unwise because even Jesus Christ warned constantly about the sinister power and deception of Satan. He informed Simon that Satan desired to sift him, meaning pull him apart. Paul said in 2 Corinthians 2:11, **Lest Satan should get an advantage of us: for we are not ignorant of his devices.** We should not be afraid of Satan if we walk in God's power and protection, but neither should we be blind sided through carelessness. Satan's power is limited. He couldn't attack Job till God permitted it, and God limited what Satan could attack, "all that he hath," but he could not take his life.

Obviously in Satan's prideful rebellion he led a group of angels with him since they are in the delegation coming to accuse Job before God in heaven. In Revelation 12:4 it says, **And his tail drew the third part of the stars of heaven, and did cast them to the earth: and the dragon stood before the woman which was ready to be delivered, for to devour her child as soon as it was born.** This is not the first time that "stars" is a cryptic, metaphorical reference to fallen angels. They are called *morning stars* back in Job 38. In Satan's original rebellion he obviously led a third of the angels with him, and they joined in murderous effort to kill the child of Mary's womb, coming from the woman of Israel. Satan failed even though Herod's slaughter of the innocent babies caused many a Jewish mother to cry out in anguish.

Satan's crime is expressed in Isaiah 14:14, **I will ascend above the heights of the clouds; I will be like the most High.** Satan wants to take the place of God. Satan wants to be worshiped. That fact is proven in the third temptation of Jesus in the wilderness. Satan could not have offered

Jesus the kingdoms of this world were it not that he had successfully stolen them from the first Adam. It took the second Adam to buy them back through a blood payment, and now the Scripture promises in Revelation 11:15, **The kingdoms of this world are become the kingdoms of our Lord, and of his Christ; and he shall reign for ever and ever.** Satan has a "kingdom of darkness," (Revelation 16:10) but that kingdom is under the control and judgment of Almighty God.

Attack and Resistance

When people think about the attacks of the devil they usually think about demon-possession. There are some fourteen cases of recorded demon possession in the New Testament. There are only three cases in the Old Testament: Abimelech (Judges 9), some prophets (1 Kings 22), and Saul (1 Samuel 16). In the New Testament the bizarre symptoms of demon possession are physical impairment that cannot be attributed to an actual physiological problem, a personality change such as depression or aggression, supernatural strength, immodesty, antisocial behavior, and perhaps the ability to share information that one has no natural way of knowing. Hollywood would add one, levitation in the air off one's bed. Because of these strange symptoms it has been widely taught that Christians cannot be demon-possessed because demons cannot live in the same house with the Holy Spirit. Did you know that is not entirely true? Did you also know that snake venom is eighty percent protein? While our bodies need protein it would be unhealthy to drink snake venom, a high source of protein, because the other twenty percent is fatal.

This is what is wrong with teaching something that is mixed with error, even if it is a small percent of error. It is agreeable that demons cannot live in the same house with the Holy Spirit, but does that mean that all Christians are immune from demon-possession? The Bible translates the word *daimonizomai* to read "possessed with devils". Literally the word means *demonized*. Can Christians be demonized? Yes, if what Paul says in 1 Timothy 4:1 is true. **Now the Spirit speaketh expressly, that in the latter times some shall depart from the faith, giving heed to seducing spirits, and doctrines of devils.** You can't depart from the faith if you were not in the faith to begin with. Admittedly not everyone who says they're in the faith are Christians, but the Bible teaches that Christians, at least in name, can and will depart from the faith and be "demonized," follow doctrines of devils, be influenced, controlled, and motivated by demons. Therefore it would be unwise for any Christian to say "I cannot be controlled by demons." Some of the worst demonic things happen between Christians in the church today.

The greatest attack of Satan and his demons on Christians today is probably **stealing our peace**. John 16:33 says, **These things I have spoken unto you, that in me ye might have peace. In the world ye shall have tribulation: but be of good cheer; I have overcome the world.** The god of this world is Satan. He will do everything he can to take away your peace. The Christian's peace is not in this world, not in this world's goods, and not in this world's pleasure. The only true peace is in Christ. When Christians have trouble, lose their things, face persecution, experience ridicule and rejection, their peace of mind and heart takes a vacation because it was not placed in the right thing–in Jesus Christ.

James 4:7 tells us that the devil can be resisted and run off. **Submit yourselves therefore to God. Resist the devil, and he will flee from you.** In all the enemy's attacks, but especially in the area of stolen peace, this tactic works to restore peace to the heart of a disturbed Christian. Submission is the first step. The word means to "put oneself under to obey." If we are hid in Christ the devil can't get at us. It is when we step outside of Christ in our own pursuits of pleasure, things, satisfaction, or recognition that we are open targets for the enemy. Quite often we are delusional to think that if we can just get rid of a certain problem in our life the peace will return. The truth is that if it were not that particular trouble that has stolen our peace it will be another. In the world you will have tribulation. Peace is not the absence of tribulation. It is the complete surrender and delight of abiding in Christ's will and protective grace that gives unassailable peace. So what do you do when peace is lost? Peter answers that question: **Casting all your care upon him; for he careth for you. (1 Peter 5:7)** The word "care" means distraction. The Christian has one purpose in life, to love, honor, obey and adore Christ. Anything that takes that away is a distraction. Are you distracted? Then you need to throw away (cast) that distraction on Jesus Christ and your peace will return. To believe that your peace is in anything or anyone other than Jesus Christ is to become severely distracted from spiritual reality.

A second way that Satan attacks is through **persecution**. 1 John 3:13 says, **Marvel not, my brethren, if the world hate you.** There is nothing more that Satan loves to do than turn people against Christians to steal their peace and joy. The world hated Him and they will hate you. It should not surprise you. The Christian should be mindful of that, watchful, and give no occasion that the adversary can use to attack us through worldly people. Even your family may misunderstand you and do you wrong. Jesus' family did (Mark 3:20-21). The answer is to love your enemies, don't cast your pearls before swine, and be wise as serpents and harmless as doves.

A third way that Satan attacks is **prayerlessness**. Prayer is our greatest weapon against the enemy, and it stands to reason it will be the prime target of Satan. Jesus hardest battle with Satan came in a garden seeking to pray in the will of God. When you do not feel like praying, pray anyway. When you are under the greatest attack turn to the One who can be your greatest Defender. The Christian who neglects his prayer life will be defeated at every turn. 1 John 4:4 is the Christian's battle cry against Satan and all his demons, **Ye are of God, little children, and have overcome them: because greater is he that is in you, than he that is in the world.**

Satan's Final Execution

First of all, Jesus Christ has already passed the death sentence upon Satan. John 12:31 says, **Now is the judgment of this world: now shall the prince of this world be cast out.** John 16:11 says, **Of judgment, because the prince of this world is judged.** Jesus did not say, "will be judged," but Satan is already judged. Colossians 2:13-15 is Paul's triumphant repetition of that death sentence:

> **And you, being dead in your sins and the uncircumcision of your flesh, hath he quickened together with him, having forgiven you all trespasses; Blotting out the handwriting of ordinances that was against us, which was contrary to us, and took it out of the way, nailing it to his cross; And having spoiled principalities and powers, he made a show of them openly, triumphing over them in it.**

Now, the question many are asking is if Satan has already been judged, defeated, and sentenced at Calvary, why does God continue to allow wickedness and evil to continue. The truth is that the human race doesn't have a right to ask that question because they already have the answer to that question in themselves. We surrendered to the temptation of sin. We raised a white flag of surrender to Satan in the garden of Eden and it was Jesus Christ who had to come buy us back and redeem this whole world from sin's curse. So, according to the Word of God it is Jesus alone who makes the decision when evil will finally be done away with. Even in our world plenty of criminals are found guilty and months pass before the trial, the sentencing, and the final incarceration. John 5:22 says that the Father has given all judgment to the Son. If Jesus Christ wants to let Satan run around this world as a usurper of power, doing evil things, that is the rightful prerogative of the Lord, and we should not question it, especially if our leaning is to fault Jesus.

Make no mistake about it, the total destruction of Satan is soon to come. The delay perhaps could be to prove the hearts of men, whether they're for God or the devil. The delay could be to bring the highest glory to Jesus in the end. The delay could be for helping Christians to be overcomers. You don't overcome anything when you don't have any trouble. Revelation 12:12 says that Satan knows his time is short. When Jesus cast out the demons from the man in the tombs at Gadara the demons said, **Art thou come hither to torment us before the time?**

The demons know they are coming to a horrific judgment of eternal damnation. When and how will this happen? First there will be the Rapture of the Church and then all hell and demonic forces will break loose in the seven years Tribulation. Revelation 20 says that near the time of the Second Coming of Jesus to the earth to rule and reign for a thousand years, called the Millennium, the angel with the key to the bottomless pit will come and chain the devil in the pit for a full one thousand years. At the end of the Millennium Satan will be loosed for a little season to go and deceive the nations into battle with God and Israel. Revelation 20:8 uses the terms Gog and Magog which confuses some about the time of this battle. Some think this is the same as the Gog and Magog battle in Ezekiel 38. It is not. There are three great battles in the end: Gog and Magog, Armageddon, and this battle of Revelation 20. All of these battles differ by time, place, conditions, and participants. This final attack of Satan against God with the nations of the world differs from the Ezekiel 38 Gog and Magog battle, because this battle encompasses all nations around the globe coming together and Ezekiel 38 is Russia coming from the north. Gog and Magog happens in the middle of the Tribulation. Armageddon happens at the close of the 7 years Tribulation just before Jesus Christ comes back to set up the Millennium, and this last battle happens at the end of the Millennium.

The interesting fact is that Satan has been bound up for a thousand years. Note that there are only three sources of temptation to evil according to the New Testament–the world, the flesh, and the devil. Only one of those will operate in the Millennium. The world will be controlled in righteousness. The devil will be locked up in the pit. Only man's flesh will tempt him. Great populations of people will flourish in the Millennium under righteous conditions, but many will only follow Christ by force proven by the fact that once the devil is let out of the pit they will follow him. Man's heart is only evil continually. He cannot save himself.

At the end of this final battle immediately Satan will be cast into the lake of fire according to Revelation 20:10. The fact that it is called "lake" means this is obviously liquid fire. We have proof of an eternal hell and a lake of fire in the heavens: White Dwarf Stars. The density of such stars as studied by the astronomers indicate that they should be 5000 times larger than they are. The reason for their small size is their temperature. At over 30 million degrees Fahrenheit at their core, the atoms are exploded separating the electrons from the proton nucleus. This is incredible because the pull of the atomic nucleus on its electrons is an octillion multiplication of the pull of earth's gravity. But at this temperature the separate parts of the atom can be compressed to such magnified density causing gases to become liquid and it never burns up. Wow, I'm glad I'm rescued from hell!!!

Reflection Station:

1. Describe how Satan came to this world and what passages of Scripture gives that story?

2. What does it mean to be "demonized," and can this happen to a Christian? (See pages 34 and 35)

3. Have you ever had your peace taken from you? Who did that to you? How did you get it back? How does the Scripture tell us to find perfect peace (Read Isaiah 26:3 and Philippians 4:6-7)?

LESSON FIVE
Doctrine of Man

LESSON TITLE: The Doctrine of Man - Anthropology

SCRIPTURE: Genesis 1:26-28; Genesis 2:1-25

TRUTH TO GAIN: Man is the marvelous work of God created to accomplish the marvelous work of God on earth.

The Highest Creation Who Took the Lowest Fall

The study of the Doctrine of Man is called Anthropology. This comes from two words: "ology" which means "the study of" and "anthropos," the biblical word for man. However, this lesson is not about the scientific approach to anthropology, as so often is the case. You can take courses in anthropology in college, and you will not receive any biblical information about man. Quite the opposite, you will study the evolution of man from apes, the physical characteristics of bone structure of human beings, and the social activities of man such as language, music, childbearing, religion, recreation, and food. True anthropology should go back to the first textbook on man, namely the Bible, to learn the truth about man's beginning and purpose from a spiritual perspective.

The Bible tells us that man is his highest creation on earth. The only thing higher in all of creation among living beings are angels, but they were not created on earth but in the heavens. Psalms 8:4-5 says, **What is man, that thou art mindful of him? and the son of man, that thou visitest him? For thou hast made him a little lower than the angels, and hast crowned him with glory and honour.** This verse tells us two significant facts. Angels are higher in the created order than man but man is higher than animals; and he is crowned with glory and honour, something that not even the angels can boast. Evolutionists seem to miss this.

The evolutionists world view is that man came from animals, which means he is just a better specimen of the same species. All that amounts to is that man is just a better monkey according to the secular scientist, Darwin's dummies. But the Genesis record clearly denotes a distinctive act of the creation of man separate from the creative acts of God in making animals. Even some theologians have made a mistake to connect man with the animals in God's creative technique. In the *Creation* magazine, Volume 4, 1981, Professor John Rendle Short wrote, "We can think of man as placed halfway between God and the animals, possessing characteristics of each. Physiologically and anatomically man is an animal. He even shares the genetic code with them. Evolutionists call him a human primate."

In the late 1800's Augustus H. Strong was a reformed Baptist and was president and professor of Biblical Theology in the Rochester Theological Seminary in Rochester, New York. Knowing that fact, it may surprise you to hear Professor Strong write in his Systematic Theology,

> While we grant, then, that man is the last stage in the development of life and that he has a brute ancestry, we regard him also as the offspring of God. The same God who was the author of the brute (animal) became in due time the creator of man. Though man came *through* the brute, he did not come *from* the brute, but from God, the Father of spirits and the author of all life.

There are three facts to note in the Genesis account which prove man did not come from or even through the brute. It can be summed up in this fashion: different dust, different day, and different destiny.

First of all, the pied pipers of evolutionary nonsense make their platform on a bed of straw when they misconstrue Genesis 2:19 which says,

> **And out of the ground the LORD God formed every beast of the field, and every fowl of the air; and brought them unto Adam to see what he would call them: and whatsoever Adam called every living creature, that was the name thereof.**

Their misguided point is that if animals were made of the ground and man was made of the dust, then they are of the same substance. Scientists even point out that they have discovered that animals and man have the same genetic code. The evolutionists are insistent that man and animal are made of carbon, hydrogen, oxygen, nitrogen, lime, iron, sulphur, and phosphorus–the same substances in various combinations which make up dirt. They even try to connect the name Adam with the Hebrew word *adamaw* which is translated ground. The truth is that these are similar words in sound but two completely different words in meaning. Adam means "ruddy" or "red". *Adamaw* means earth, ground, soil. Now unless Adam came from Tennessee red clay there can be no justifiable connection.

The first thing that needs to be understood is that the animals which were earth beasts were begun on day five and man was created on day six. Secondly, even though the beasts of the earth were created on day six man was created after the beasts, separate from the beasts and from different dirt. The word *ground* and the word *dust* are totally different in the Hebrew Bible. Finally, nowhere in the Bible does it say that God breathed into the nostrils of an animal and they became a living soul. Nowhere in the Bible does it say that God ever made a baboon, monkey, or ape in the likeness or image of God. Man may have some of the most common elements of the soil such as carbon, nitrogen and phosphorus just as animals, but to make that an argument for man being a higher manifestation of an animal is like saying Oscar Mayer bologna is just the beginning form of a T-bone steak.

Man truly is a unique creation of God. Psalm 139:4 says, **I will praise thee; for I am fearfully and wonderfully made: marvelous are thy works; and that my soul knoweth right well.** What does it mean for man to be made in the image and likeness of God? The simplest explanation is that there are created characteristics in man that are in likeness to the nature and essence of God. However, this must not be taken too far to say like the cults and false religionists that man is a little god, or is becoming a god. "Likeness" and "equal" are two different things just as fried catfish and fried chicken are two different things even though both are fried.

There are at least five characteristics in man that are in the likeness of God, which no animal has or ever will possess: language, creativity, love, holiness and immortality. First of all, animals do not possess the ability to learn, formulate, and express **intelligent communication** across the palate and tongue through grammatically correct vocabulary in sentence structure. You may be thinking of animals that do know how to communicate. Dolphins use radar, follow hand signals, and can be trained to mouth sounds responding to signaled commands, but that is not language. Birds make sophisticated sounds and even parrots can apparently say words mimicking what they have heard, but this is not intelligent language for we have never heard a bird answer a question on the game show Jeopardy.

Have you ever heard of the "waggle dance?" Honey bees do that. If a honey bee finds a field of flowers and he can't bring all the pollen and nectar back himself he will fly back to the hive and have an animal communication with his fellow workers. He will incredibly use the position of the sun as his fixed point reference, turn his body around in the direction away from the sun he wants them to go, and then wag his behind the exact number of times in bee feet or yards that it takes to get to the flower where the pickup is to be made. Aren't you glad that God didn't leave your communication skills to your behind?

The human brain for communication skills is absolutely exhibit A for God's amazing creative work in man. How does it compare to a desktop computer. Most computers today hold about 1-10 Gigabytes of information on the hard drive. A Gigabyte is one billion bits of information. Scientists have estimated the human brain has about 100 trillion neurons and each neuron holds one bit of information. So already we have a human brain that is a thousand times the storage capacity of the average one gigabyte computer. But scientists go on to tell us that each neuron has 50,000 synapses, each believed to hold a bit of information which now multiplies this 50,000 times 100 trillion neurons giving us 50 x 10^{18} which they call 500 terabytes. A terabyte is equal to 4000 gigabytes. The final calculation by a computer scientist says that the human brain will store twenty-four petabytes of information. That is almost twice what the world's largest supercomputer in Russia will store. And this human supercomputer walks on two feet and doesn't have to be stored in a large warehouse.

Language comes from the processing center of the brain. Animals are missing their processor in the language department. The day a pig can tell you it is a pig will be the day it ceases to be a pig. It's a puppet named Miss Piggy and somebody's hand inside her head wagging her cardboard mouth.

Creativity–it is the ability to think and make things. Dogs can watch man all day build a campfire but they will never be able to build one themselves to stay warm out in the cold. The Bible says that when the tabernacle was being first built in the wilderness that God filled a man named Bezaleel **with the spirit of God, in wisdom, and in understanding, and in knowledge, and in all manner of workmanship** to shape metal and carve wood for the ornate building of the tabernacle structure and furniture. Yet a spider endlessly designs the same monotonous style of web, and the bird has never built an insulated birdhouse with running water. Beavers build a dam but it is the same structure of a pile of sticks. Animals cannot reason but only respond to external stimuli and threats to their existence.

Animals do not know what **love** is. They know what animal attraction is and a male dog can smell a female dog in heat five miles away, but it is not love when he goes courting the neighbor's hound. 1 John 4:16 says **God is love.** But God doesn't lick you in the face. Animals may show cute responses, conditioned responses to their owners that seem to be affectionate, but it is nothing like the capacity to love given to the heart of man in creation.

God tells us in 1 Peter 1:16 that He is **holy** and tells us to be holy. Man has the capacity to seek and worship God. Animals do not. When is the last time you saw a cow folding its hoofs together out in the field and praying, "Dear Lord and Creator, for this alfalfa hay I'm about to chew I am thankful?" For man to be created in the image of God means that there is a part of man's makeup that compels him to seek out and worship his creator. There is a God-sized hole in his heart and no man will be truly fulfilled in life till he fills that hole with the pursuit of God.

Finally, man is **immortal.** Genesis 2:7 says, **And the LORD God formed man of the dust of the ground, and breathed into his nostrils the breath of life; and man became a living soul.** That soul will live on in eternity. Death is not the end. Job said it well when he declared, **But man dieth, and wasteth away: yea, man giveth up the ghost, and**

where is he (Job 14:10)? Job knew that man must be somewhere after death, but he wasn't quite sure in what form that would be. David said of God in Psalm 102,

> **Of old hast thou laid the foundation of the earth: and the heavens are the work of thy hands. They shall perish, but thou shalt endure: yea, all of them shall wax old like a garment; as a vesture shalt thou change them, and they shall be changed: But thou art the same, and thy years shall have no end.**

God is everlasting, existing outside of time, and his days are forever. Jesus said the same would be true of man. In John 5 he tells his disciples, **Marvel not at this: for the hour is coming, in the which all that are in the graves shall hear his voice, And shall come forth; they that have done good, unto the resurrection of life; and they that have done evil, unto the resurrection of damnation.** The Bible never says animals have a soulish existence. But the breath of God in man allows him to move out of the body and into eternity somewhere.

With all this crowning glory in man's creation, it is the most heart-wrenching story that man was given freedom to choose to live a perfect, everlasting, sinless life in the very beginning in the garden of Eden, yet he chose to break the will of God and die in his clay house. God's word says that Adam sinned and so death has passed upon all men. Christians do not die. They just go to sleep. Sinners die eternally. What is the extent of sin's effect upon man.

The Effect of Sin

In the doctrine of man we believe that the Fall of Adam and Eve has passed on the drop of sin's curse into the bloodstream of the human race. Romans 5:12 is the primary verse that tells us this fact. **Wherefore, as by one man sin entered into the world, and death by sin; and so death passed upon all men, for that all have sinned.** Some may say that this is not fair because it was not your personal decision to take the forbidden fruit, and you should not suffer for Adam's sin. The fourteenth verse of Romans 5 says that death has come upon all men even if they have not sinned **after the similitude of Adam's transgression.** We may have not sinned the same sin that Adam sinned, but the Bible teaches that all men are sinners by nature and by choice. It is our nature from birth to be given to sin. Psalm 51:5 says, **Behold, I was shapen in iniquity, and in sin did my mother conceive me.** We are also sinners by choice. James 1:14 says, **But every man is tempted, when he is drawn away of his own lust, and enticed.** We cannot blame anybody else for our sin because it is truly self motivated and activated. The reason for this is what is called total depravity. Total depravity means that sin has corrupted the whole person– the emotions, the will, and the intellect. Jeremiah 17:9 says, **The heart is deceitful above all things, and desperately wicked: who can know it?** That's the emotions. Because of sin you can't trust your heart to do the right thing. You can choose to do the right thing with the power of Christ in you, but your heart will always push you to do the wrong thing.

The Apostle Paul spoke about the will being weakened by sin. **For that which I do I allow not: for what I would, that do I not; but what I hate, that do I....For I know that in me (that is, in my flesh,) dwelleth no good thing: for to will is present with me; but how to perform that which is good I find not (Romans 7:15, 18).** Not only are the emotions and will affected, so is the intellect. That is your mind. John 6:44 says, **No man can come to me, except the Father which hath sent me draw him: and I will raise him up at the last day.** Man cannot even make up his mind to follow Christ unless the Father draws him. Romans 7:23 says, **But I see another law in my members, warring against the law of my mind, and bringing me into captivity to the law of sin which is in my members.** The flesh, that part of man which is forcing its selfish will, wars against the mind that hears the law of God and knows he should obey. But because of sin the conscience can become dull, the body is dying every day molecule by molecule, the spirit is dead unto God without being quickened by the Holy Spirit, and we are totally and personally guilty before God as sinners.

Does all this mean that we have lost the image of God due to sin? No, we would say the image has been defaced, but not erased. The image was obviously not totally gone because of sin because then man would have lost his immortality, creativity, communication, love, and any desire for holiness. The image of God in man can be restored through a new birth and a new life. **Therefore if any man be in Christ, he is a new**

creature: old things are passed away; behold, all things are become new (2 Corinthians 5:17). The moment that a person receives Christ the image is restored because Hebrews 1:3 says that Christ is the "express image" of the Father. That is why Colossians 1:27 says it is "Christ in you" which is the "hope of glory." Remember that God's original intention in the creation of man was to crown him with honor and glory. That only happens as man exalts His Creator.

So what are the signs that a sinner has been saved and the image is restored. The experience of God's grace causes **SIN TO LOSE DOMINION** in the Christian. Romans 6:14 says, **For sin shall not have dominion over you: for ye are not under the law, but under grace.** Secondly, the restored image produces a **RENEWED MIND**. Ephesians 4:23-24 says, **And be renewed in the spirit of your mind; And that ye put on the new man, which after God is created in righteousness and true holiness.** Saved sinners have a constantly changing mind to desire righteousness and true holiness in their lives. They have come out of darkness into the light. They are putting away evil things because they truly desire a right relationship and fellowship with God. Thirdly, a restored image causes the **CREATIVITY AND WORSHIP IN MAN'S HEART TO BE TOTALLY GOD-CENTERED**. Some Christians, believe it or not, think that getting drunk or taking drugs is creative. That is the devil's lie. Some Christians think that Christian lyrics put to the rock music of the world is creative. That is the devil's lie.

Creativity without holiness and purity is rebellion. Some people just use God to better their image. There is nothing good about our image. Psalm 39:5 says that **man at his best state is altogether vanity.** That word *vanity* means "useless." Only God's image restores man to life. To make God do it our way is not Christianity but religiosity, and there is not one religion in the world that will get us back to God. Religion is what man does for God. Christianity is what God does for man. Man does not merit any of the grace of God. Any religion of works, rituals, duties, or performance to gain God's favor is a fool's endeavor. Man finds his "best state" when he surrenders to and rests in the grace of God.

From Here to Eternity

Man is on a journey through a short life to a unfathomably long eternity. What is our purpose in life? What will be our position in eternity? Perhaps the best verse to ponder in reflecting on those questions is a question Jesus raised one day while here on this earth. **For what is a man profited, if he shall gain the whole world, and lose his own soul? or what shall a man give in exchange for his soul (Matthew 16:26)?** The verse before that says, **For whosoever will save his life shall lose it: and whosoever will lose his life for my sake shall find it.** The verse before that says, **If any man will come after me, let him deny himself, and take up his cross, and follow me.** Sometimes it is good to read the word of God backwards and you will discover great answers to great questions.

God created Adam and Eve in perfect innocense without the shame or guilt of sin. They flagrantly ignored the warning of God and violated their freedom to choose in life when they chose disobedience–something they wanted rather than something God wanted. The result was they lost their life. They lost the garden. They lost their dominion. They lost their innocense. They lost their peace because working in a thorn-cursed earth, fighting the adversary Satan for the rest of their lives, and bearing children in sorrow is no peace at all.

One of the things that man, even redeemed man, hasn't learned yet is that there is absolutely nothing in this world worth clinging to. It is all fading and falling apart. That is what Jesus meant when He said you would lose your life if you tried to save it. His alternative was to take up your cross and follow Him. We are on a journey toward a celebration for all eternity of Christ's redeeming work in our lives. That's why Philippians 3:20 says, **For our conversation is in heaven; from whence also we look for the Saviour, the Lord Jesus Christ.** The word *conversation* is really citizenship, the Greek word *politeuma*. If our citizenship is in heaven then we are foreigners in this earth and we should be looking to get back home. Also the only reason for our existence here and now is to prepare for our return trip to glory. Foreigners can't wait to get back home. When they are in a foreign land they stock up on the things they'll need when they get back to where they call their real home. Can you think of the things we will need in heaven? Could it be the ability to worship well, the record of holy living and dedicated service to the King of Heaven for a good reward at the Judgment Seat, the love of the spiritual rather than the material, the joy of a family reunion, the knowledge of Christ, and perhaps the appreciation of Christian fellowship. Christians are going to spend more time off of earth than on it. We sure need to be getting ready. We plan so much to live. What about planning to die? There is a heaven to gain and you don't have to wait till you get there to incorporate the heavenly citizenship in your earthly life.

Reflection Station:

1. If someone said to you that the animals according to the Bible came from the ground and Adam came from dust, and so, evolution is a valid principle, how would you refute their logic by the Scripture? (Three facts in the Genesis creation narrative)

2. Give some characteristics in man that indicate he is "made in the image of God."

3. If one of the reasons for our existence is to prepare for our return trip to our real home, how do you prepare for heaven?

LESSON SIX
The Doctrine of Salvation

LESSON TITLE: The Doctrine of Salvation - Soteriology

SCRIPTURE: Acts 4:12, Hebrews 2:3, Psalm 8:4

TRUTH TO GAIN: Man in his sinful depravity doesn't deserve to be saved, has nothing in himself to gain his salvation, and must totally rely on Jesus Christ to remove his sins and save him from eternal death under the wrath of God. The only right and decent response to salvation is total surrender to God's will.

The Right Questions

A lesson on the doctrine of salvation is rightly place immediately after a lesson on the doctrine of man. You cannot understand the desperate need of salvation without understanding the reality and consequences of man's sinful condition. The doctrine of salvation is called Soteriology. This word comes from the Greek word *soteria* for salvation. The angel announced that a Savior, a *Soter* was born in the city of David. *Soter* means the one who rescues and delivers from certain destruction. Have you ever asked yourself these very important questions? Why should God who is completely Holy, all powerful, all knowing, and totally self-sufficient ever desire to save sinners? Furthermore, why should He subject Himself to the pain of losing His only Begotten Son to death in order to save people who rebelled against God's goodness? This question perplexed David and he wrote in Psalm 8:4, **What is man that thou art mindful of him.**

Peter and John had spoken the power of God into the lame man's body for healing. That lame man got up and walked. In fact, Acts 3:8 makes a point to say he was not only walking but leaping and praising God. For such a miracle, all three responses give adequate gratitude for the grace of God. Peter and John use that background miracle to tell the critical religious rulers of the day that the means of the miracle is Jesus, and the purpose of the miracle is to declare the message of salvation. Nothing is more impotent, lame, crippled, helpless than a soul condemned because of sin. But there is good news. **Neither is there salvation in any other: for there is none other name under heaven given among men, whereby we must be saved (Acts 4:12).** The Christian as well as the sinner needs to understand the impact of the saving work of Jesus Christ.

The Demands for Salvation

When Peter says "whereby we **must** be saved," he is preaching the urgency and necessity of salvation for every living soul. There are three unchangeable facts that present the demands of salvation: 1) the **depravity of man pleads salvation**, 2) the **death of Christ provides salvation,** and 3) the **holiness of God prescribes salvation**. Looking at all three shows the amazing grace of God to make it possible for anybody to be saved.

Under the doctrine of man you discovered that man is a sinner by nature, by choice, and by declaration. He is born into sin as a part of the race of Adam. He makes conscious choices to rebel against God. And if man will not recognize that he is a sinner by nature and by choice, he must recognize that by declaration God calls him a sinner; and to deny that is to call God a liar. God says in Romans 3:23, **For all have sinned, and come short of the glory of God.** What this means is that there is nothing in man that qualifies himself or enables himself to save himself. He is utterly lost and hopeless to turn his sinful condition around. If man had a thousand years to live or a thousand lifetimes to repeat he would mess all of them up with sin. His good deeds do not for any moment outweigh his transgressions against God anymore than one rotten egg thrown into the bowl of six bright yellow eggs would make a good omelette for breakfast. Man, for the most part, is a deceived, optimistic fool if he looks at his life and thinks his record is not all that bad. God hints in Isaiah 64:6 that our best estimates of ourselves falls far beneath the estimate of God. **But we are all as an unclean thing, and all our righteousnesses are as filthy rags; and we all do fade as a leaf; and our iniquities, like the wind, have taken us away.**

God alone decides about our eternity. He has already decided that for everybody. Unless you are saved from sin, His way, you will die forever in hell separated from Him in endless torment. So, the depravity of man pleads salvation. Considering the desperation of our depravity, it is a wonder why sinners are not beating down the church doors to get to the altar of repentance.

Secondly, the death of Christ provides salvation. It is difficult for the finite human mind to understand how a death, any death, is needed to provide life and salvation. The closest we can come to understand it in the natural realm is that a woman comes as closest to the door of death when she gives birth to a child; or when someone donates an organ of their body at the risk of their own life to save another. Yet, this does not even come close to what Jesus did for our souls.

To answer the question of why death for salvation and why Jesus' death, of all people, for salvation you have to go to Hebrews 9:22, **And almost all things are by the law purged with blood; and without shedding of blood is no remission.** Unlike man, God takes sin seriously, prescribing lawful and unavoidable penalties for sin. The writer of Hebrews says that according to God's law "almost all things" require blood shed to pay the penalties for man's sin. Read Leviticus 5:11-13 and Numbers 16:46; 31:50 to discover there are only five sins not purged with blood to satisfy the requirements of the law: 1) witnessing a foolish, unkept oath and not exposing it, 2) touching and defiling one's self with uncleanness from an animal or human, 3) swearing a reckless oath that cannot or should not be kept, 4) complaining against God's servants for the justifiable acts of God's punishment, and 5) receiving war spoils and divine protection for soldiers unworthy of the gracious acts of God. For these sins the requirement to purge them was a grain offering, fire from the brazen altar offered up with prayer, and jewelry. Everything else was purged by blood.

Why is blood required to cover sin? Blood is a symbol of life. Leviticus 17:11 says, **For the life of the flesh is in the blood: and I have given it to you upon the altar to make an atonement for your souls: for it is the blood that maketh an atonement for the soul.** Now it was not the physical shedding of blood alone that saved us. If that were the case then Jesus could have just bled a little instead of dying. It was His dying by shedding His blood that saved us. People make wills of their estate before they die but that will and testament cannot go into effect until the person is dead. God cannot die. He is eternal. So two things had to happen in order for God to save us. The Savior of mankind had to be able to die to save us, and He also had to be God, a sinless sacrifice, in order for that death to be an effective payment for our sins. Jesus was born of a virgin mother, was fully God in human flesh, lived a sinless life, and thus died as the perfect sacrifice for the penalty of our sin. To recap: sin brings death; blood brings life.

Now thirdly, the holiness of God prescribes salvation. There is only one prescription for the deadliest disease known to man, the disease of sin. The holiness of God has to be satisfied in order for God to cover sin, and the wrath of God has to be appeased (bring back to a state of relief, to quieten, calm, or ease) in order to stop the just punishment against all men for their sin. You may be thinking how could a loving God feel this way. He is not only loving. He is holy. The Bible says in Habakkuk 1:13 that His eyes are so pure He cannot even look upon evil. We are also told that He is the judge of all the earth and He will do right. (Genesis 18:25; Exodus 34:7). A payment for sin had to be made. It was either salvation or annihilation. This payment had to be paid by a sinless sacrifice because God could only accept atonement for sin from an unblemished sacrifice. There had to be a way to change our relationship with God from hostility (the Bible calls it "enmity" in Ephesians 2:16) to harmony and peace. There was a way, praise God! Romans 5:1 says, **Therefore being justified by faith, we have peace with God through our Lord Jesus Christ.** The demands of salvation are narrow, prescribed, and exacting, so much so that Matthew 7:14 says, "few there be that find it."

The Three Tenses of Salvation

Salvation is past, present and future according to the Bible. We are saved from sin's penalty, the curse of eternal death and separation from God. That is salvation past, something that is already done. This is called **redemption**. Jesus said on the cross, "It is finished." This is why it is so dangerous to add anything to the work of Christ at Calvary as acceptable to God to save your soul. We are not saved by our works, our goodness, our merit, our personal accomplishments, or our associations. We are saved by God's grace alone through Jesus Christ. It is important to note that these three tenses of salvation are not three different **methods** of salvation, but really three ongoing **manifestations** of the one great salvation through Christ. If you have one, you will have them all.

Salvation is not only past but also present. We are being saved daily from the dominion of sin. Sin does not have to have power over our lives because of Christ's power within us. Romans 6:14 says, **For sin shall not have dominion over you: for ye are not under the law, but under grace.** Whereas salvation past is called redemption, salvation present is called **sanctification**. Romans 5:10 says, **For if, when we were enemies, we were reconciled to God by the death of his Son, much more, being reconciled, we shall be saved by his life.** That verse has to be speaking of two different accomplishments of Christ's work on the cross: reconciled by his death (that is past) and saved by his life (that is present).

Too many Christians are ignorant or act ignorant of the fact that Christ's saving work covers the whole journey between conversion and death or the return of Christ. Because of this they live compromised, defeated, hypocritical lives. Salvation present is being saved not from the presence of sin, because that won't happen till we get to heaven. However, salvation present is being saved from the power of sin. Sin does not have to get power over your life and control your living anymore if you are in Christ. How is that possible? We are saved by his life. When a person gets saved He takes Christ into His heart. Paul said, "for me to live is Christ." It is no longer our life that is being lived out. It is the life of Christ in us. We have died. We are not in control anymore. Salvation is doubly good because it rescues us from death and releases us from the grip of sin. We are saved from the guilt of sin and the government of sin.

Thirdly, salvation is future. We are not only saved from sin's penalty and sin's power. We are saved from sin's presence. This is **glorification**. Two verses wonderfully make this plain. Paul wrote in Romans 13:11, **And that, knowing the time, that now it is high time to awake out of sleep: for now is our salvation nearer than when we believed.** This is talking about something that is coming in the future, our going to heaven. Hebrews 7:25 says, **Wherefore he is able also to save them to the uttermost that come unto God by him, seeing he ever liveth to make intercession for them.** When will we get to the uttermost part of salvation? When we come into the presence of Jesus Christ, then and only then, will we have exchanged the corruptible for the incorruptible. When mortality shall have put on immortality, when the sinning nature will be completely laid aside for the likeness of Christ, we will be free totally from the power and presence of sin. What a day that will be when my

Jesus I shall see! At that point the source and the seductiveness of sin will be removed completely. Do you long for that day?

We have discussed three tenses of salvation but there is one more tense of salvation that must be recognized. It is outside the past, present or the future. You could call it the "dateless past." Eternity exists outside of time and everybody needs to know that the salvation of a man's soul was never an afterthought with God nor a part of future planning. It was in the mind and heart of God all along. Revelation 13:8 says Jesus Christ was **slain from the foundation of the world.** What does that mean? Before man was even a speck on the earth, God's son was dying on a cruel cross in the eyes of a loving Father who did not want any man to perish. How thankful are you for that?

The Vocabulary of Salvation

There are several words in the scriptures that speak of the work of God in our salvation. In the original languages of the Bible these words speak graphically of what Christ did for us at the cross. First of all there is **CONVERSION.** Peter preaches in Acts 3:19, **Repent ye therefore, and be converted, that your sins may be blotted out, when the times of refreshing shall come from the presence of the Lord.** The Greek word for conversion is *epistrophe* a compound word of *epi* meaning "above" and *strophe* meaning "twisting or turn around." It has the idea of another Person acting upon you to completely turn you around. One definition says "revolution." There are folks who claim to be saved but they do not turn around. In this fact it is dangerously possible to believe you are saved and safe when all the while you are lost and unchanged, on your way to hell. This explains the drastic change spoken about in 2 Corinthians 5:17.

RECONCILIATION. 2 Corinthians 5:19 says, **To wit, that God was in Christ, reconciling the world unto himself, not imputing their trespasses unto them; and hath committed unto us the word of reconciliation.** This word reconciliation, *katalasso* in the Greek, means to restore to Divine favor through mutual change. When we are saved we are restored in God's favor by our change and God's change. God changes from wrath to mercy. Man changes by repentance and belief in Christ. It is Christ who is the Mediator in the middle bringing the Father and the sinner back into fellowship. God cannot change if we will not reverse our position concerning sin once and for all with a life decision for Jesus. Another way to conceptualize reconciliation is that man repents and God relents. Man turns away from a life of sin, and God turns away from His holy wrath against sin. We have changed and God has changed. The only reality is God's change is completely within His divine attributes. He is both merciful and just. His justice has to be satisfied before mercy can be applied.

REDEMPTION. Ephesians 1:7 says, **In whom we have redemption through his blood, the forgiveness of sins, according to the riches of his grace.** The word is *apollutrosis* in the Greek. The word means a release from captivity because a ransom has been paid. The ransom that has been paid is the blood of Jesus.

SUBSTITUTION. 1 Peter 3:18 says, **For Christ also hath once suffered for sins, the just for the unjust, that he might bring us to God, being put to death in the flesh, but quickened by the Spirit.** Man cannot save himself because he cannot suffer the eternal torment as the just penalty for his rebellion against God. Jesus did it for us and lived beyond the grave. He took our place. Bible commentators refer to this as the substitutionary or vicarious death of Christ. Vicarious means the sufferer sympathizes with the one for whom he suffers. There is a connection between the two. In the Old Testament the sinner would bring an animal sacrifice, lay his hands on the head of the animal, and then kill the animal for sacrificial atonement for sin. The animal took the place of the offerer but the offerer had to touch the animal for it to be any good. The reason why man cannot be his own Savior by any sacrifice he may bring is that such sacrificing never ends and is never finished. Christ, once for all, became our substitute and finished the work of atoning for our sins (Hebrews 10:10).

ATONEMENT. Romans 5:11 says, **And not only so, but we also joy in God through our Lord Jesus Christ, by whom we have now received the atonement.** Atonement means to cover and to cancel the debt. Animal sacrifice in the Old Testament covered the sins of the people till the death of the Lamb of God could cancel the debt. It is often said that Christ brought us back into "at-one-ment" with God.

PROPITIATION/EXPIATION. Romans 3:25 says, **Whom God hath set forth to be a propitiation through faith in his blood, to declare his righteousness for the remission of sins that are past, through the forbearance of God.** This Greek word for propitiation is *hilasterion*. It is the same word used for the mercy seat on the ark of the covenant. Jesus Christ is that mercy seat, that place upon which the wrath of God fell for our sin, and purchased the mercy of God for our forgiveness. While the word *expiate* is not in the Scripture it is a word that Bible scholars use to relate the idea of removing guilt. So expiation is removing the guilt off the sinner, and propitiation is removing the wrath of God from the sinner.

JUSTIFICATION. Romans 5:1 says, **Therefore being justified by faith, we have peace with God through our Lord Jesus Christ.** In Bible language, *dikaioo* is a legal term meaning "acquittal from all the charges against a person." With the slap of the gavel on the judgment bench of God, the Father is able, because of the death of Christ, to declare all believers "not guilty but instead legally righteous in the eyes of God." This makes 2 Corinthians 5:21 so sweet. **For he hath made him to be sin for us, who knew no sin; that we might be made the righteousness of God in him.** There are other words connected with the doctrine of salvation which are worthy of the students investigation such as impute, forgiveness, repentance, sin, grace, mercy, faith, adoption, election, and regeneration to name a few. The diligent Bible student will give time and attention to them all.

The Only Acceptable Result of Salvation

At this point it is worthy to examine the result of our response to the saving work of Christ since we have studied the result of the work of Christ for us. What should happen in the life of a person who is truly saved? Read Exodus 21:1-6. In today's society of abortion, drive-by shootings, domestic homicide, abandonment of the elderly, and cultic-enforced suicide it is apparent the human race has forgotten mercy. But God sought to write in the fabric of Hebrew culture and their laws a timeless testimony to the mercy and grace of God. In this Exodus 21 passage a man might buy a Hebrew to be his slave, but he could only force him to serve him for six years. The seventh year was the year called Jubilee. It was a year of freedom. Slaves were set free. Debts had to be canceled. It sure would be a strange thing if in America all debts were canceled every seven years. One might think that a person in such case would amass all the debt he could and then get off paying it in the seventh year. That wouldn't happen because there would be fewer cases of lending if the lender knew the debt couldn't be liquidated in seven years. At any rate this law was for the betterment of society.

The slave, in the year of Jubilee, had two choices. He could go free and take his own wife and kids with him without any further forced slavery. If the slave owner during the time of his owning the slave had provided a wife to the slave, that wife and any of her kids had to stay and serve the master. But in a strange turn of options, God said the freed slave might decide that he likes, even loves his master. His master has been good to him, and so he decides he wants to stay in that relationship. Such a decision is not for six more years, or ten years, or twenty years. It is for life, and had to be sealed with a puncture wound, a mark of ownership in the slave's ear. The master would take a sharpened bone or stick, take the slave and hold his ear up against the doorpost, and run it through with the piercing tool. Blood would run profusely from the ear. A hole would be left permanently in the ear so that all who looked on that slave knew his choice to stay with his master.

This is a perfect picture of true salvation. We go from bondage to freedom, and then to bondslavery to the Master. It is a willing choice. It is a permanent choice. It is a visible choice. Paul says in Romans 1:1, **Paul, a servant of Jesus Christ, called to be an apostle, separated unto the gospel of God.** That word servant is *doulos* in Greek and literally means bondslave. It is a bond produced by overwhelming love. There is nothing like it in any other religion. Christ sets us free from the curse of sin, and the evidence that we have received Him and His forgiveness of the debt is that we consciously choose to turn in our freedom papers, take the adoption papers, and file the separation papers from the world. It is a decision to accept the gospel and to serve Jesus forever from a heart of unquestioned and loving obedience. Anything less is not true salvation.

Reflection Station:

1.	What is the name given to the Doctrine of Salvation?

2.	Explain what we mean when we speak of the depravity of man?

3.	What attribute of God demands payment for sin?

4.	Match the terms of salvation with their correct definition.

1. Conversion	A. Cover and cancel the debt
2. Reconciliation	B. Jesus took our place to suffer
3. Redemption	C. A release from captivity
4. Substitution	D. Acquittal from all charges
5. Atonement	E. To be turned around
6. Propitiation	F. Mercy seat
7. Justification	G. To restore to Divine favor

LESSON SEVEN
The Doctrine of the Church
Part One

LESSON TITLE: The Doctrine of the Church: Part One - Ecclesiology

SCRIPTURE: Matthew 16:13-19

TRUTH TO GAIN: The Church of the Lord Jesus Christ is a blood bought institution and deserves our respect, faithfulness, involvement, humble service, sacrificial giving, and cooperation in the Great Commission.

The Origin of the Church

In Matthew 16:18, Jesus Christ gives the defining clue to the origin of the church. He did not say that He would add to something that was already in existence. He said He was beginning something new, although it was not new in the mind of God. It was new in the history of man. There is an interesting mind twister: "Did it ever occur to you that nothing ever occurred to God." God knows everything. God has everything planned out. God in his wisdom never has something to just occur to His mind, and then, on the spur of the moment decides to do it. The Bible says of God in Isaiah 46:10 that He is **declaring the end from the beginning, and from ancient times the things that are not yet done, saying, My counsel shall stand, and I will do all my pleasure.** So, the Church was in the mind of God all along but it did not begin till Pentecost.

Why is Pentecost the birthday for the Church? Four reasons: 1) Ephesians 1:20 says that Jesus Christ was raised from the dead so that He could sit at the right hand of the Father. This position makes Christ, according to Ephesians 5:23, the ruling Head of the Church. Therefore, the Church would have had no head before the resurrection, making it impossible for the establishment of the Church prior to the resurrection; 2) Ephesians 4:7-12 tells us that it was Christ's ascension which provided Him with gifts to give unto believers for the operation of the Church. The Church could not have been a functioning entity with any ability to "edify the body of Christ" without these gifts, and that did not come till after the ascension; 3) In Ephesians 3:3-6, Paul says that he is showing a revelation of a mystery that had been revealed to him. He says that mystery is the fact that Gentiles can become the fellow-heirs of the body of Christ along with believing Israelites. Romans 16:25 says this mystery had been kept secret since the beginning of the world. The mystery is the Church, the joint body of Jews and Gentiles who receive the redeeming grace of Jesus Christ. Before Abraham, believers would be called the "family of God." From Abraham to Pentecost believers would be called Israel. Then all believers since Pentecost are called the Church; then finally 4) The Church could not exist prior to the giving of the Holy Spirit for indwelling. Pentecost is the birthday of the Church because Pentecost marks the promise of Christ to send the Holy Spirit in John 14:17 who **dwelleth with you, but shall be in you (John 14:17).**

The word *church* comes from the Greek word *ekklesia* which literally means the "called out ones." The word *ekklesia* refers to a called out or called together assembly of people. In the New Testament it doesn't always have a religious meaning. In Acts 19, there was an uprising against Paul in Ephesus for frustrating Demetrius the silversmith in the idol worship of the goddess Diana. This was a political assembly which met illegally trying to bring charges against Paul. But most often in the New Testament the word *ekklesia* for church is a reference to the local church or churches in an area.

The word *ekklesia* appears 115 times in the New Testament. Except for three occasions where it is translated "assembly" it is always a reference to the word church, a spiritual gathering of believers. Ten times the word *ekklesia* refers to the universal church in the world, the whole body of believers around the world. Over one hundred times the word refers to the local church. This is important because people who say they can be a Christian without belonging to a local church are confessing their ignorance of the Bible and their disobedience to Christ.

Sometimes you will read in the Apostle's Creed and other documents such phrases as the "holy catholic church" and the claim is asserted that it refers to the universal church of believers from the time of Adam till the end of time. There is a danger in using this phrase for two reasons: 1) it becomes confused with the Catholic church denomination which according to Scripture is the mother of harlots deceiving people with their false doctrine and salvation by church sacraments; it is a sacrilege to have any loyalty to that system of beliefs if you are a New Testament believer; 2) not everyone who says they are a believer in the world is truly a believer because Jesus says you're only a part of his family if you do His will (Matthew 7:21 and Matthew 12:50).

So, if *ekklesia* means a called out assembly, where did the English word *church* come from? It comes from the Anglo Saxon word *kirk* and the Scottish word *kirkus*. There is humor in the Scotch word because it is where we get our word "circus" and the church sometimes really is a circus. But that word is a reference to something round, in that circuses were done in three rings inside a tent, something round, and some of the oldest temples and churches were built in the round. There are a lot of churches going "round and round" like the Hebrews did in the wilderness. Christ said to Peter that upon his confession, not upon Peter, not upon the Pope of Rome who claims to be the authorized Vicar of Christ under Peter, and not upon any creed of any church, the Lord will build His church. It is built upon the profession that Jesus is the Christ the Son of the Living God. Jesus alone builds His church. Men do not build His church. Programs do not build His church. Money does not build His church. Prominent people do not build His church. **Except the LORD build the house, they labour in vain that build it (Psalm 127:1).**

The Officers of the Church

In the New Testament there are five words used for servants in the church: bishops, elders, deacons, deaconness servant, and a prophetess. The question is to which ones of the five are recognized officers of a New Testament church. It is easily explained from Scripture. A bishop and elder are the same office. How do we know that? The word "elder" is used 67 times in the New Testament and the word "bishop" is used 4 times, once referring to Jesus Christ. They are two different words in the Greek language, bishop being *episkopos* and elder being *presbuteros*. But is it possible that they are the same office in the church with notable functions from the same leader? It is apparently clear that they are the same officer by four arguments from Scripture. Number one: In Titus 1:5-7, Paul told Titus to appoint elders in every city in Crete and then immediately called them bishops. Number two: In Acts 20:17, 28 Paul called for the elders of the church of Ephesus to meet him at Miletus and he described their position as "overseers" which is the same word for bishop, *episkopos*. Number three: When Paul lists the qualifications for the officers of the church in 1 Timothy 3 he only mentions bishops and deacons. We know there were elders in the church so why didn't he mention them? He didn't need to mention them if they were one in the same with bishops. Number four: Again in Philippians 1:1, Paul mentions bishops and deacons but not elders. If there were three classes of leaders why didn't he mention all three. It would have been an oversight otherwise if it were not for the fact that bishops and elders are the same office.

There is no question among the denominations as to the fact that deacons are ordained officers of the church. What is debated is their function and their authority. Some churches give the deacons charge over the financial matters of the church. This is a grave mistake and unbiblical even though it is argued that they were given charge of serving tables in Acts 6 which meant buying the food. It is a stretch of the most biased mind to claim Acts 6 is a warrant to make the deacons financial officers and administrative overseers. The primary mistake is in the fact of ignoring their title, deacons. *Diakonos* means servant. Their service was clearly appointed by the apostles as indicated by Acts 6:3 which says, **Wherefore, brethren, look ye out among you seven men of honest report, full of the Holy Ghost and wisdom, whom we may appoint over this business.** The New Testament is clear to show the authority of pastors over deacons, not the other way around. It is the common wreckage of many modern day churches when deacons forget the reason for their office, and begin to feel the pride of their position to the point of ruling the church and make their pastor subservient to their wishes. They will answer to God in judgment and punishment for such wickedness in the church.

That word "business" in Acts 6:3 is the Greek word *chreia* which has the meanings: employment, occasion, demand, or need. The obvious meaning of the appointment of deacons is that there are occasions of service where a demand or a need in the church must be met in order to free up the pastor's time for studying the Word of God and prayer. The deacon is employed in service for this need. This in no way makes him a boss, an authoritative officer of the church, or a big shot to walk pridefully among the congregation. On the contrary, by nature of his office and function he should be one of the humblest men in the congregation.

But the question remains: Are there supposed to be women deacons in the church? Some make the case for this by one passage of Scripture, Romans 16, where Phoebe is referred to as a "servant" which is the Greek word for deacon. There are two reasons why no church should ever ordain women as deaconesses. First, if Phoebe was an official deaconess at Cenchrea, she is the one lone case in all the New Testament and in all the first century as such. It would be strange that she alone would hold the office of a deaconess and nobody else if this was a recognized office for women in the first century Church. Secondly, if Paul had meant to indicate she was an official deaconess he would have used the feminine article or the feminine form of the noun in Greek for deacon, but he didn't. There is a great need for women workers in the church but 1 Timothy 2:12 says that a woman is not to "usurp authority over a man." Though deacons have no authority, except that which is given by the pastor and the church, a woman is not to take the place where a man is called to serve.

What about prophetesses? It is true that Anna in Luke 2:36 was a prophetess. It is also true that Philip the evangelist did have four daughters which according to Acts 21:9 "did prophesy." But are these official offices of the church? No! They were functions of women believers in the first century who were very close to the Lord. Anna was a widow of 84 years old who spent all twenty-four hours of her days in the temple fasting and praying. No wonder she was able to be a prophetess. The word literally means someone who foretells the future. There is no need to foretell the future today because Christ has come and He is our future. We have His word about the future and need no other. Now, the gift of prophecy is still operative but distinctly operates under divine inspiration to "forth-tell" the Word of God, not foretell the future. The only two recognized offices in the church today are bishop/pastor and deacon.

The Ordinances of the Church

The ordinances of a New Testament Church are baptism and the Lord's

Supper. In the Catholic Church they are called sacraments and they have seven: baptism as an infant, confirmation, the Eucharist (Lord's Supper), penance (confession of sin and restoration through holy acts such as hail Marys with the rosary beads), holy orders (ordained as a priest, monk, or nun), matrimony (no marriage outside the Catholic church is recognized, and if so you are excommunicated), and extreme unction (last rites at death done by a priest to get you into heaven). Catholicism has raped the New Testament with their tradition.

An ordinance is something that is ordered by the Lord for the Church to do. A sacrament is defined by the Catholic church all the way back to the time of the Council of Trent from 1545-1563 as "something presented to the senses which has the power, by divine institution, not only of signifying, but also of efficiently conveying grace." For this reason, we reject the term sacrament to be applied to either Baptism or the Lord's Supper. Neither one can convey grace. They picture grace, but they cannot give grace. Catholics say some hocus pocus words in Latin over the wafer in the Lord's Supper and they believe it literally becomes the physical body of Jesus, and the wine literally becomes the blood of Jesus all over again. This is the doctrine of Transubstantiation. We reject such nonsense and divination, and refuse therefore to use the word "sacrament."

Baptism is required of all believers but it does not save the soul. 1 Peter 3:21 says it is the "answer of a good conscience toward God." Baptism is an act of obedience and refusal to do it is to have a bad conscience for disobedience. It very well could be that the disobedient person is not a believer at all. With rare exception everyone in the New Testament that got saved was baptized. Jesus demonstrated it as a righteous act (Matthew 3:15-16). The Philippian jailer was baptized and his whole house. Does this mean infants in his house were baptized? Certainly not, because we would be jumping to conclusions in the first place to assume that he had any infants. Secondly, the Scripture order of salvation is always believe and then baptism. It is impossible for infants to follow that order because they have no mental capacity to believe till they come to the age of accountability.

Baptism is clearly by immersion into water. It is impossible to accept any other method of baptism and be scripturally sound for four reasons:
1) At Jesus' baptism, according to Mark 1, the Lord went into the water and came up "out of the water,"which cannot mean anything other than immersion. The same is said for the Ethiopian eunuch's baptism even in the desert. (Acts 8:36-39); **2)** The Greek word *baptizo* has the specific meaning to "overwhelm and make fully wet". The Greek New Testament has other words for sprinkle or pour and never uses these for baptism; **3)** Baptism, according to the New Testament, has always been associated with the death, burial, and resurrection of Jesus Christ. You can't get that picture properly with sprinkling or pouring; and **4)** There was never a case in the New Testament where baptism was administered by anything other than immersion. Historical documentation proves that there were hundreds of pools in or around Jerusalem where they could baptize three thousand souls from Pentecost if several of the apostles were performing the task. It is also interesting to know that the Eastern Greek Orthodox Church, who has used the Greek language since the first century, have always baptized by immersion.

Another cardinal truth about baptism is that it does not save the soul. This heresy is called baptismal regeneration. It is believed by Catholics and the Churches of Christ. One verse suffices to prove it wrong. It is a verse used falsely by the Churches of Christ to claim baptismal regeneration. Mark 16:16 says, **He that believeth and is baptized shall be saved; but he that believeth not shall be damned.** If baptism saves you Mark left out a critical phrase in that verse. It should read, "He that believeth and is baptized shall be saved; but he that believeth not *and is not baptized* (Emphasis mine) shall be damned." But Mark is careful to say that the only thing that damns the soul is unbelief, not failure to be baptized.

The privilege of partaking of the Lord's Supper follows the ordinance of baptism. This is revealed in Acts 2:41-42. There is a divine order there. Baptism precedes the "breaking of bread." The Lord's Supper is not mystical or magical. It is simply a memorial. Jesus Christ said in Luke 22:19 to do the Lord's Supper in "remembrance" of Him. The Lord's Supper is an ordinance to call to mind the great sacrifice Christ made for our sins. We are never told in Scripture how often to do it. We are just told "how" to do it–"in remembrance." Therefore, the frequency with which we observe the Lord's Supper should never be so often that it loses its impact on our ability to freshly meditate on Christ and the crucifixion. Some people want to do it often because they believe it puts them more in favor with God. There is no truth in such belief.

The Corinthian church abused the Lord's Supper in three ways: **1)** They were not discerning the Lord's body which meant they were apathetic to the costly sacrifice of Christ for their souls; **2)** They were not examining themselves to rid themselves of their strife and divisions in the congregation; and **3)** They were concentrating more on the feast of food at the ordinance rather than the sacredness of the memorial. A thorough observation of 1 Corinthians 11 shows that the common love feast which was observed with the Lord's Supper was abused by acts of gluttony and hoarding personal food brought to the feast and not sharing with the poor. Paul told the Corinthians to eat at home. This is not a total prohibition of eating in the church or Baptists would be in trouble with constant disobedience in their fellowship meals. This is a contextual thing with Corinth to forbid them from making the Lord's Supper a sacrilege.

When should the Lord's Supper be observed? To be accurate it should take place at least part of the time in the evening service since it is referred to as a "supper." Then, it also should remain in the church, not taken outside, since 1 Corinthians 11:18-20 speaks of "coming together" into "one place." The Greek word *sunerchomai* means "with the assembly." Taking it to the nursery or to nursing homes or to individual homes steps outside of the New Testament practice, and often reflects the mistaken belief that it is a sin to miss the observance.

Should the Lord's Supper be taken by visiting Christians in an established assembly? This raises the issue of "open communion" or "closed communion." Some churches open it up to all believers and some churches close it to just the local church membership. We are not told in the New Testament exactly how to handle this issue. Each church should decide. Two factors affect the decision. One is that local church discipline is connected with the Lord's Supper as illustrated in the Corinthian church situation. This would seem to confine the observance to the local church because you would never know about outsiders if they were properly observing the supper or in need of discipline. But what are you going to do, refuse the ordinance to a visiting saint? And how do you ever know completely a man's heart? Numbers 9:14 may lend some light to the issue since there is a specific detail mentioned in the observance of the Passover.

> **And if a stranger shall sojourn among you, and will keep the passover unto the LORD; according to the ordinance of the passover, and according to the manner thereof, so shall he do: ye shall have one ordinance, both for the stranger, and for him that was born in the land.**

According to the New Testament the Lord's Supper was instituted out of the Passover. God said that if a stranger wanted to observe the Passover with Abraham's tribe they could do so as long as they did it the prescribed way. There was to be one ordinance for the stranger and for the one born in the land. The only requirement was that the stranger had to be circumcised. Circumcision was a physical ritual that symbolized a spiritual reality. It signified a bond of loyalty and love to Jehovah God. There should be no soul that is not circumcised in heart, born again, saved by the grace of God, ever permitted to observe the Lord's Supper.

Reflection Station:

1. Is the Doctrine of the Church called Ecclesiology or Eschatology?

2. Explain why a "bishop" and an "elder" are the same office in a New Testament church?

3. Explain why it is improper to call the Lord's Supper by the term "sacrament."

4. Explain why proper baptism must be by immersion in water.

5. **True or False**

   Partaking of the Lord's Supper often puts a person more in favor with God.

LESSON EIGHT
The Doctrine of the Church
Part Two

LESSON TITLE: The Doctrine of the Church: Part Two - Ecclesiology

SCRIPTURE: Ephesians 5:27 and 1 Timothy 3:15

TRUTH TO GAIN: The work of the Church is never haphazard or self-serving. The New Testament gives decent and orderly instructions for a glorious operation of God's institution. The Church should be the greatest trophy of the strength of God and the purpose of God on this earth.

The Operations of the Church

The operations of a New Testament church include the government and the guidelines. There are four types of government in churches of today: **1) Minimal government** where the church is ruled by several elders, several ministers lead the congregation, spiritual gifts and spiritual discipline are highly regarded, and church membership is downplayed. Groups like the Quakers and the Plymouth Brethren practice minimal government. **2) National government** is where the church is ruled by the powers of the political state such as the Anglican church in Europe and the Lutheran church in Germany. **3) Heirarchical government** is where the church is ruled by a file and rank of clergy with specific titles indicating their level of authority. The Methodist church and the Church of God operate loosely under this type of government, but the Episcopal and Catholic churches are strict examples of heirarchical government. The people of these churches have less say of the matters of the church than the leaders. **4) Congregational government** is where the ultimate authority over the church rests in the membership of the church. This is usually applied through democratic processes. Most protestant congregations follow this type of government.

There is one major flaw with congregational/democratic government. It is not truly biblical. Democracy is the invention of man dating back to the sixth century B.C. among the Greeks. From the time of the Garden of Eden, God ruled by virtue of the fact that He is Creator. He delegated dominion to Adam over the earth. From that time till the days of Samuel, some 2,800 years later, this form of government existed as the standard till the people decided to adopt a congregational approach and request a king. They did not like the authority of the delegated few over the many. This was a challenge to the shameful acts of Eli the priest. Samuel, the prophet, was quite upset with the people's request but God told him in 1 Samuel 8:7, **For they have not rejected thee, but they have rejected me, that I should not reign over them.**

The era of the kings was a blight upon the nation of Israel because it was a rejection of theocratic government. Theocracy means the rule of God in whatever way He so chooses. In the days of Moses, Korah, Dathan and Abiram challenged the theocratic rule of God through Moses. They said, **Ye take too much upon you, seeing all the congregation are holy, ...wherefore then lift ye up yourselves above the congregation of the LORD?** The result of that rebellion was disastrous with the loss of many lives cast into the bowels of the earth. Congregational government is a disaster waiting to happen.

In the Baptist Church Covenant it says, "we will cheerfully recognize the right of the majority to govern." In the Baptist Faith and Message, a confessional document of the Southern Baptist Convention, Section VI under the topic of The Church, reads as follows: "Each congregation operates under the Lordship of Christ through democratic process." The only thing that is right in that statement is the words, "Lordship of Christ." But if Jesus Christ is Lord there will not be a democratic process. Why? Because democracy involves people rule and people rule is decided by voting which is foreign to the New Testament. You will never find a case of voting in the New Testament. Even in Acts 6 it was not a vote, but a "choice" under the administration of the apostles.

Obvious reasons explain the absence of voting in the New Testament record. Without mentioning the numerous references to Scripture God always presses the church to be of one mind and one accord. Two examples are cited. In Acts 6 it says that deacons were chosen but did they vote? No, because it says in verse 5, "the saying pleased the whole multitude." There was a unanimous consensus of the apostle's authoritative leadership and no vote was needed. This action was not initiated by the congregation, no motion was made in a business meeting, but quite differently the apostles under the leadership of the Spirit suggested it, and the congregation unanimously in one accord stood with the decision. So there was congregational involvement but not congregational jurisdiction.

Acts 15:22 states, **Then it seemed good to the apostles and the elders, with the whole church, to choose men from among them to send to Antioch with Paul and Barnabas.** No statement of voting appears in this record. There was consensus as they talked about all the questions involved. But the lines of theocratic authority are established clearly in the passage, naming the apostles and elders first, followed by the statement, "with the whole church." It is evidence of an elder-led church.

Too many congregations grievously had rather follow Robert's Rules of Order rather than God's Word of Truth. They had rather adhere to the "majority rules" philosophy than Hebrews 13:17 which says, **Obey them that have the rule over you, and submit yourselves: for they watch for your souls, as they that must give account, that they may do it with joy, and not with grief: for that is unprofitable for you.** Voting more often than not can never reach a consensus, a one-mindedness. It is a trap for human opinion, and we must not forget that there are many scriptural examples where the "majority" were dead wrong such as in Noah's day. The government of the church should be a perfect unity under the Headship of Jesus Christ operated through His divinely ordained leaders. These leaders must not lord it over the flock, but have a servant-spirit. Jesus said, **He that is great among you shall be your servant.**

The guidelines of a New Testament Church are crucial for prosperity and blessing. Ten guidelines are primary: **1)** The Scriptures are the complete and exclusive guide for the church's operation. (2 Timothy 3:16-17);
2) The pastor of a church must be a called man of God. (Hebrews 5:4);
3) Jesus Christ is the Bishop and Shepherd of our souls as well as the Head of the Church (1 Peter 2:25 and Ephesians 5:23); **4)** Membership of the church is always through the door of salvation (Acts 2:41); **5)** The Church's ministry comes by means of the priesthood of every believer operating in Spirit-given spiritual gifts (Revelation 1:6 and 1 Corinthians

12:4-12); 5) **6)** The means of support to the Church's ministry is the cheerful, regular and systematic giving of tithes and offerings by its members (Malachi 3:8, Matthew 23:23, and 1 Corinthians 16:1-2); **7)** The Great Commission of reaching the lost for Christ is not an option but a command, only successful through Spirit-leadership, faithful obedience to go out and share the good news of Christ, and holy living to back it up (Matthew 28:13-20 and Titus 2:12); **8)** New Testament churches should extend the Kingdom of Christ around the world, each member responsible to the best of his/her ability to spread the gospel to all nations, an endeavor we call missions (Luke 24:47); **9)** Intelligence of the Scriptures should be the norm of all church members, not the exception (2 Timothy 2:15, Matthew 22:29, Acts 17:11, Romans 15:4, 2 Timothy 3:15); and **10)** The New Testament Church attitude should be one of complete adoration of God, radical denial of self, categorical love of all, and sweeping commitment to serve Christ (Matthew 22:37, Matthew 10:39, Matthew 5:43-48, and Mark 9:35)

The Objectives of the Church

What is God doing with His Church in this world? The Scripture offers us some provocative answers to that question. These answers may clearly indict the churches of this age that they have adopted their own agenda and mocked the Lord of the Church in His purposes. First of all, the church is the **meeting ground for joyful worship**. Psalm 100 is wonderfully familiar to the Christian.

> **Serve the LORD with gladness: come before his presence with singing. Know ye that the LORD he is God: it is he that hath made us, and not we ourselves; we are his people, and the sheep of his pasture. Enter into his gates with thanksgiving, and into his courts with praise: be thankful unto him, and bless his name.**

One of the saddest commentaries on the modern church is that better than eighty percent of America is unchurched, and perhaps so because of lost joy or pseudo joy in today's worship services. Worship is the adoration of God, not the adoration of a performance for God. Many churches today have their bands and their popular music which does more for exalting man than exalting God. True exaltation of God never needs to adhere to a particular style of music in order to effectively facilitate heart-felt worship. It is the words in a song, not the notes in a song, or the beat in a song that becomes the fitting vehicle into the presence of God. Yet man has evolved backwards to the time of Aaron and the golden calf at the base of Sinai, feeling that the frolic of the emotions supercedes the holy honor of the truth about God. Joyful worship is never carnal to feed the fleshly desires. Joyful worship ascends the stair steps of praise in direct proportion to the familiarity with God. This is why Psalm 96:9 says, **O worship the LORD in the beauty of holiness: fear before him, all the earth.** To be truly familiar with God is to fear Him. Out of that fear comes profound and free flowing gratitude for the amazing grace given to our lives.

The church is the **pleading ground for God's miracle power**. The single most rewarding activity of the church today has to be prayer. By prayer comes the mighty acts of God to rally the church on in her enterprise. By prayer Peter was set free from prison. By prayer demons were routed into the drowning depths, setting an otherwise hopeless man free from destructive forces. By prayer leaders were chosen that prospered God's work. By prayer doors for the gospel were opened that otherwise would have remained ever so closed. By prayer sickness was banished. By prayer hardened sinners were saved. By prayer death was turned back. By prayer enemies are defeated. By prayer the fire of God falls, so says Elijah. The church must not be caught in the web of complacency about prayer, for if she does it will be said of her she has a "form of godliness" but contradicts the power of God in her foolish indifference.

The church is the **breeding ground for world evangelization**. The pulpiteers of the land must be hot on missions and cold on carnality, not the other way around. There should be the environment of old in the church today where many are being called to preach and called to the mission field. Jesus prayed in John 17:18, **As thou hast sent me into the world, even so have I also sent them into the world.** Jesus had one purpose when He came to this world–to save souls. Why is it that the church today has lost that compelling drive that was in the Master's heart "to seek and to save them that are lost?"

The church is the **completing ground for a spotless bride**. Paul says in 2 Corinthians 11:2, **For I am jealous over you with godly jealousy: for**

I have espoused you to one husband, that I may present you as a chaste virgin to Christ. Jude 24 also says, **Now unto him that is able to keep you from falling, and to present you faultless before the presence of his glory with exceeding joy.** Finally, John the Revelator says, **And I John saw the holy city, new Jerusalem, coming down from God out of heaven, prepared as a bride adorned for her husband.** The Church is the bridal dressing room where preparations are being made to come adorned in purity for the Bridegroom who comes out of heaven for his chaste virgin. The question is what is the church doing today to get a clean wedding garment for that Marriage Supper of the Lamb?

The church is the **reading ground for angelic education**. A strange verse for sure appears in Ephesians 3:10, **To the intent that now unto the principalities and powers in heavenly places might be known by the church the manifold wisdom of God.** The word "intent" expresses purpose. The "principalities and powers" is a consistent reference to angels. That phrase "by the church" means the church is the agency by which this God ordained purpose can be accomplished. God purposes to use the church to educate the angels in the eternal plan of God for the ages of time. We have another hint of this heavenly scheme in 1 Peter 1:12,

> **Unto whom it was revealed, that not unto themselves, but unto us they did minister the things, which are now reported unto you by them that have preached the gospel unto you with the Holy Ghost sent down from heaven; which things the angels desire to look into.**

What are you teaching the angels about the ways of God? The church is the showcase of God's wisdom not only to this world but also to the high creatures of the next world.

The church is the **bleaching ground for dirty saints**. Churches don't practice church discipline anymore. Why is that? It is because a "little leaven leaveneth the whole lump." It has infected not only the pew but also the pulpit. Preachers by the hundreds are being caught in sexual immorality. The New Testament strongly warns of our responsibility to

have no fellowship with the unfruitful works of darkness, but rather reprove them (Ephesians 5:11). Paul told the Corinthians that they were too proud to deal with a sinning saint in their congregation that was living with his stepmother. He told them they had no choice but to purge the man out of their congregation. Paul even said that church discipline must be exercised publicly against a sinning preacher but not without reputable witnesses to the sin. He wrote in 1 Timothy 5:20, **Them that sin rebuke before all, that others also may fear.** God wants to use his church as a purification plant. He desires that strict discipline of unrepentant sin be the lightning rod of fear in a congregation. There is no better place on earth to learn the fear of God than in the church.

The church is the **preaching ground for an undebatable Book**. It must be the most loved, most practiced, most enjoyable, and most stirring experience of the saint's gathering–the preaching of God's Word. We do not come to church to share human ideas. We do not come to church to find a self-help philosophy to better our life on earth. We come to hear a word from God, and you can't get that word outside the Bible. The gospel enterprise began with an uncompromised preacher preaching righteousness, John the Baptist. The call of the disciples separating them from the world and their secular occupations was for nothing less than to preach repentance and faith in Christ. It was preaching that saved 3,000 souls at Pentecost. It was preaching that saved the Ethiopian eunuch in the desert. It was preaching that brought Lydia, a rich woman to Christ, not an offer to sit on the finance committee. It was preaching, according to Titus 1:3, that properly manifests God's Word. Preachers should not piddle behind the pulpit. They should speak, "thus saith the Lord," or go home. The church must not succumb to the pressures of the world to secularize their agenda and shelve old-fashioned preaching for godless substitutes.

Finally, the church is the **leaping ground for Heaven**. Nothing else in life should excite the saint more than for the prospect of the Lord's soon return to gather His children. Titus 2:13 says, **Looking for that blessed hope, and the glorious appearing of the great God and our Saviour Jesus Christ.** The Rapture of the church is a blessed hope for expectant saints, but an undesirable interruption for distracted saints. The key is in that word "looking." It means to confidently and persistently be watching. Jesus told the church to "watch and be ready." Instead she is missing her objective when she is distracted and dirty. Many will be caught by surprise like a thief that has come in the night. 2 Timothy 4:8 says, **Henceforth there is laid up for me a crown of righteousness, which the Lord, the righteous judge, shall give me at that day: and not to me only, but unto all them also that love his appearing.** The Church of the Lord Jesus Christ is to astound the world by one thing if by nothing else, their upward gaze. Are you looking and longing for the coming of the Lord?

Reflection Station:

1. For what reasons should a person attend a local church regularly?

2. Which is more important in the church, the organization or the objectives? If the organization is not helping the church meet the biblical objectives should the organization be changed? When should the organization of a church not be changed?

3. What percentage of America is unchurched?

4. Should churches practice New Testament discipline of wayward Christians by going to them and rebuking sin while lovingly calling them back to faithfulness to Christ?

The Doctrine of the Bible

LESSON TITLE: The Doctrine of the Bible - Bibliology

SCRIPTURE: 2 Timothy 3:16-17, Psalm 119:89, 2 Peter 1:21

TRUTH TO GAIN: Despite all critical attacks, the Bible has proven itself to be the literal inspired Word of God without error and is worthy of our reverence and obedience.

The Shocking Questions

Perhaps the doctrinal study of the nature of the Bible should be the very first lesson in a series like this, but the author takes for granted that a student of doctrine would accept the Bible as the authoritative source for all teaching. This is not always the case. Plenty of young men and women have left good Christian homes to study in secular schools or even religious institutions where liberal professors have undermined their faith and trust in the Bible. Without a solid foundation of faith in the accuracy of the Bible as God's Word, the unsuspecting student is easy prey for the broad-minded, open-minded, and we should say empty-minded attacks against the Bible in our neo-pagan world.

Have you ever been asked or confronted with any of these questions: **1)** How do we know that the Bible is God's Word? **2)** How do we know that the Bible is not just some writings by fallible human beings? **3)** Aren't there errors in the Bible because some passages seemingly contradict others? **4)** Which parts of the Bible are literally true and which parts are just fictional stories to illustrate a lesson? **5)** Isn't it alright just to accept the message of Christ and salvation without worrying if there are errors in the Old Testament? Then the harder questions come: **1)** Who decided what books belong in the Bible? **2)** What about the so-called "lost books" of the Bible? **3)** When Paul wrote 2 Timothy 3:16 that all Scripture is inspired of God , 2 Peter, Hebrews, Jude, and all of John's writings were not even written yet. Does that make them uninspired? **4)** How do we know the Bible is inerrant since we don't have any of the original manuscripts? These are questions which produce three different responses.

Some defend the Word of God even to the point of complete ignorance. In the days of Joshua (Joshua 10) the great warrior for Israel commanded the sun to stand still and God's word says the sun and the moon both stood still. Scientifically we know for a fact that the sun and the moon do not move anyway. It is the earth that revolves and rotates around the sun. But well-meaning preachers have claimed through the years that if it says the sun stood still that meant that it stopped from moving. Such a defense of Scripture is not needed to the degree of foolishness. It appeared to the writer of Joshua that the sun was moving.

There is a second group that just accepts that the Bible has errors and to them it does not matter for whatever measure this authority of the Bible is challenged. "The Bible has errors - so what," they would say. This crowd believes the principles of the Bible is all that matters whether the Bible is completely truthful or not. Then the question becomes who is qualified to sort out what are the inspired principles and what parts are in error?

Then thirdly, there is a group that puts the Bible side by side with other scriptures like the Hindu Bible - the Bhagavad Gita, or the Koran, or the Book of Mormon. They would say each book is a valid philosophy book for personal religion holding equal truth. All three of these responses are irresponsible, dangerous, and foolish when you examine the true nature of the Bible - Genesis to Revelation. The scriptures do not need a poor defense as in the first case. The scriptures, if they have error, are suspect to any value in the principles of teaching since they could not be trusted for truth. If any part of the Bible is in error than all is suspect. Finally, the scriptures are infinitely more worthy than the Bibles of any false religion.

The First Issue: Inspired Means What?

The first concern is to know what the Bible means when it says it is inspired. Did God reveal His word supernaturally by dictation? Did He allow the writers to research information and write from the freedom of their own personal expression? Or did God pick men with such genius of mind to write His book that they did not need any supernatural help? To answer these questions there is one word in 2 Timothy 3:16 that will shed great light on the subject. The word "inspiration" is *theopneustos* in Greek. This word is a compound word with two meanings: God and breathed. The Scripture is God-breathed. God used human writers but He breathed into the activity of their writing our sacred Bible. That means God was in charge of their thinking, their choice of words, the length of the writing, the purpose of the writing, where these books were written, and where they would go. At no time did God ever take a back seat to the project of bringing to the world sacred Scripture. This fact shuts down the critics claim that the Bible was just written by men.

Another consideration of chief importance is that Peter says it was not just any men chosen to write God's book. 2 Peter 1:21 says it was *holy men of God*. In fact, Peter boldly declares that the Word of God did not come by the will of man. A true understanding of inspiration believes God directed all of His writers of Scripture in every word they chose to pen on the parchments of those original manuscripts. They **spake as they were moved by the Holy Ghost.** That word "moved" is the Greek word *phero* which means "carried along." If you will read Acts 27:15 you will find the same word "moved," which is illustrated by a ship that Paul was on in his third missionary journey, a ship that couldn't be controlled due to a fierce wind. They "let her drive" which meant the wind took that ship wherever it wanted to blow. The ship was carried along and the passage implies that God was doing it to accomplish His sovereign purpose. In the same way the writers of the Bible were carried by the guiding force of the Holy Spirit to record exactly what God wanted recorded in the Bible. If the Bible had been subjected to their personal wills it no doubt would have been full of errors and uninspired. But God directed their wills and used them to do His perfect work.

Now, some people say the Bible is inspired in spots. But what man on earth is inspired enough to spot the spots? This is sometimes called "Partial Inspiration" or "Degree Inspiration". What this leads to is the idea that when the Bible speaks about salvation we can trust it, but when it speaks about historical information there are errors. The truth is that salvation is based upon historical facts, and if there are certain historical facts in the Bible that are in error, how can we trust any of the historical facts, including those about salvation. In other words, if Jonah didn't historically get swallowed by a huge fish and was spit out after three days still alive, then how do we know we can trust the Bible when it says Jesus was in the tomb for three days and arose from the dead on the third day?

Some folks believe the Bible is inspired because spiritual geniuses wrote it. They did not need any supernatural help for God to breathe out His Word because they were able to do it on their own. But would we call David who committed adultery with Bathsheba a spiritual genius? Would we call Amos, a sheepherder and fig-picker, a country preacher whose language didn't come anywhere close to the glorious language of Isaiah, would we call him a spiritual genius? Would we call Jeremiah, who wished he hadn't even been born, a spiritual genius? Holy men of God were God's instruments, but they were also fallible and feeble. If it were not for God's superintendence over the work of Scripture we would not have a trustworthy Bible. Why is it that geniuses today cannot write such Scripture that prophesies the future and sways the heart to be saved?

Some people believe that inspiration means the thoughts are inspired but not the words. This is foolish thinking because you do not get thoughts without words. If the words are in error then the thoughts have to be in error. Through this ignorant claim people will say that the **intent** of the Bible is inspired but not the **content**. Have you ever known a car engine to run perfectly where the parts are faulty? How would you like a surgeon to say to you before the operation, "Uh, we don't know exactly what is wrong with you; we don't know what part of the body is malfunctioning; we don't know how to set up the operating room and what instruments we will use, but we are absolutely positive you need surgery and are quite certain this procedure will come out alright and you will live." Often the folks who have this view of inspiration call it "concept inspiration." Their concept of the concept is in error. Jesus Christ Himself said, **Man shall not live by bread alone, but by every WORD that proceedeth out of the mouth of God.** He did not say we live by the principles, the concepts, or the thoughts. We live by the words, *rhema* in the Greek, which means individual and specific utterance. Every word of the text from Genesis to Revelation is God-breathed. If you do not believe in verbal inspiration of the Bible you do not have a trustworthy Bible from a trustworthy God.

The Second Issue: Why Must We Claim Inerrancy for the Bible?

It is important to understand that inspiration leads to inerrancy. The Bible cannot have any errors simply because God is the author of the Scriptures. Jesus Christ Himself said in John 10:35, **The scripture cannot be broken.** To believe there is one error in the Bible is to claim that God cannot be truthful, and Titus 1:2 says that God "cannot lie." Now, follow this out. Someone says there is an error in the Bible, just one. Is that really so bad, just one? What if there are twenty opinions on where that error is, and so, now you have as many as twenty errors if it is in different places. Then if there are as many as twenty errors, there might be a hundred. Even if there are twenty or a hundred the question becomes how can you trust the Bible at all if it has a few errors. Then some Bible professor or scholar points out that the only thing we can claim inerrancy for is the original manuscripts; and since we do not have any original manuscripts inerrancy doesn't matter. It does matter! Since all we have is a copy of the original Word of God are we going to say we don't have an inspired Bible? If so, we have no authority source to promise us salvation, heaven, forgiveness, or even a God who listens to our prayers. That would only be available to those who had the original manuscripts of the Bible to be sure that the Word could be trusted.

Jesus said in Matthew 5:17-18, **Think not that I am come to destroy the law, or the prophets: I am not come to destroy, but to fulfil. For verily I say unto you, Till heaven and earth pass, one jot or one tittle shall in no wise pass from the law, till all be fulfilled.** Do you know what a jot or tittle is? First of all, Jesus is promising that the law and the prophets, basically the entire Old Testament, is guaranteed to be fulfilled. It is inerrant according to Jesus. The "jot" is the Hebrew letter *yodh*. It is the smallest letter in the Hebrew alphabet. It is about the size of an English apostrophe and looks a lot like the apostrophe. Jesus is saying that letters make words, and words make thoughts in a sentence, and thoughts and sentences make promises. He is claiming for the Word of God that not even a letter in a word of God's word will ever fail.

You can change letters in a word and totally change the word. The word "tough" changes to "touch" when you change the "g" for a "c" and both the word and thought totally change. Jesus said that God will make sure that no matter what errors man may make with God's word the Word of God will not change, will not be hindered even though there is a misspelling or a mistake in the copy. The Hebrew "tittle" is smaller than the "jot". The Hebrew letter *kaph* can be made into the Hebrew letter *beth* with a little tittle on the bottom right of the letter. But when you change that letter you change the word. The Hebrew word *kad* means pitcher. But if you change the *kaph* (the "k" in *kad*) to a *beth* by making just a little squiggle curl mark on the bottom of the letter, Genesis 24:14 would totally change. Abraham had sent his servant Eliezer out to find a bride for Isaac and the test would be that out of all the women who came to the well the one who offered to draw water for the camels also when the servant asked her to get water out of the well for him would be the bride for Isaac. But just change the one letter *kaph* to *beth* by a little, near-microscopic mark in the Hebrew, and you have the verse reading "let down thy linen britches" rather than "let down thy pitcher." Jesus was saying that even the littlest details like that, regarding the reliability of Scripture, are watched over by God Himself. Psalm 119:89 says, **For ever, O LORD, thy word is settled in heaven.** The issue of inerrancy is settled in heaven, not on earth.

So, what about the supposed errors people find in our Scriptures today such as Numbers 25:9 and 1 Corinthians 10:8? Moses records in Numbers that 24,000 people were killed because of their worship of Baal. But Paul refers to the same incident in Corinthians saying 23,000 were killed. Is that an error? Not if you read the whole verse in Corinthians. Paul says "in one day". Moses likely was including additional deaths in subsequent days. What about the question of who killed Goliath? 1 Samuel 17 says David killed Goliath but 2 Samuel 21:19 says a man by the name of Elhanan slew the brother of Goliath but the phrase "the brother of" is in italics in the English version which means it does not appear in the original Hebrew. The English translators have added those words to clear up the apparent discrepancy. Are the English translators covering up a real error in the Scriptures? Do they have a right to add words to cover up a supposed error in the Word of God? No, they added those words to the Hebrew because 1 Chronicles 20:5 clearly tell us that Goliath's brother was named Lahmi and Elhanan did kill him.

There are perhaps a hundred other examples of pinpointed errors raised by the critics of the Bible such as how did Judas die–by hanging or by falling headlong and his bowels gushing out; Were there two blind men healed at Jericho or just one named Bartimaeus according to Luke and Mark; Was the mustard seed really the smallest seed or was Jesus saying something that was untrue; or where did Cain get his wife if nobody was around but his sisters and God opposes incest? Those who support the doctrine of inerrancy say that all errors clear up when you understand the language of the Bible or further research reveals facts that clear up any hint of error. The truth is that if you come to the Bible with a view that there may be errors you will probably find them, but if you come to the Bible with confidence that it is a God-breathed word you won't be shaken by any problem raised by the critics. It only takes one error to make the Word of God suspect but Peter says we have a **more sure word of prophecy (2 Peter 1:19).**

The Third Issue: Who Decided the 66 Books?

What about the lost books of the Bible? That is a question that worldly people pitch around today to dislodge God's claims upon their life by laying a dull axe at the tree of Scripture. In 1546, the Catholic Council of Trent claimed that fifteen other books belonged in the Bible, a group of writings commonly called today *The Apocrypha*. These books do appear in the Catholic Bible called the Latin Vulgate. The names of the books ought to be a dead giveaway that such should not be in the recognized God-breathed Scripture, but you just can't drill the truth into some heads with a Milwaukee drill or a jack hammer. This is why Paul writes in 2 Thessalonians 3:2 that the Thessalonians might pray that he would be delivered from unreasonable and wicked men: "for all men have not faith." Books like 1st and 2nd Esdras, Tobit, Judith, the rest of Esther, Ecclesiasticus, Bel and the Dragon, Susanna, 1st and 2nd Maccabees, and the prayer of Manasses in the Apocrypha do not pass the test of true scripture from God.

There are books called the Pseudepigrapha, a word that means "writings falsely attributed," and they have titles like 1st and 2nd Enoch, Testaments of the Twelve Patriarchs, Life of Adam and Eve, and the Book of Jubilees. These books should not be in the Bible for good reasons? First, none of these books claimed inspired authorship such as Moses, the lawgiver, or one of the called prophets of God. Second, for four centuries not one of these books were ever accepted by the Jews as a part of the Bible. Third, though there are 264 quotations of the Old Testament in the New Testament, not one of them comes from an apocryphal book. Jesus never quoted from the Apocrypha or the Pseudepigrapha. These so-called lost and found books support lies and false doctrine such as purgatory, praying for the dead, prayer to idols, and worship of angels. In the two books of Maccabees, which is only a historical account of the Jews fighting for freedom from Greek rule through a heroic Jewish warrior named Judas Maccabeus, there are inconsistencies. These books have the enemy king, Antiochus Epiphanes dying three different times, three different ways, and in three different places. Talk about errors! Another reason they don't belong in the Bible is they don't talk about salvation. Fifthly, they make offensive claims which do not represent God's truth. Ecclesiasticus 25:19 says that any sin is insignificant beside the sin of a wife and Ecclesiasticus 22:3 says it is a loss to a father to sire a baby daughter. Sixthly, these books teach lying, suicide, assassination and magical incantation. Finally, a seventh reason is that they contain numerous historical and geographical errors.

So how did we come to get our sixty-six accepted books of the Bible as inspired? These thirty-nine books of the Old Testament and twenty-seven books of the New Testament are what is called the *canon* of Scripture. That word *canon* comes from a Greek word that means a measuring instrument. In other words, the canon of Scripture is that which measures up to the rules for inclusion in the sacred words of God. Some people again find fault with the Bible saying that men decided what books would be in the Bible. This is really not true. Men didn't decide what books would be in the Bible anymore than they decided to write the Bible. God called men to write it and God directed men to just recognize what books fit the test, fit the rule of God-authored Scripture.

By 397 A.D. the Christian Church had clearly declared that the canon of Scripture was closed with only sixty-six books fitting the test. What were the guidelines that measured the books to see if they were Scripture? **Number One**: True scripture had to claim the penmanship of a patriarch, prophet, or apostle connected with God or the authority of such leaders of Israel backing the real human author of the book (such as Peter who was the source for Mark's gospel). **Number Two**: The books had to demonstrate unmistakable evidence of inspiration by the Holy Spirit. **Number Three**: The books had to be predominantly accepted by the Christian Churches. No books were included in the canon that were doubted by any large number of churches to be inspired from God. **Number Four**: The books had to demonstrate a supernatural effect upon the heart of the reader bringing a transforming moral change into the life of the readers. **Number Five**: Some search was made for external evidence such as archaeological evidence that would validate the book. Though the canon was closed in 397 A.D., the discovery of the Dead Sea Scrolls in 1947 produced over 900 fragments of ancient manuscripts. Forty percent of those 900 fragments were copies of Old Testament books confirming Scripture to be authentic. So, in the truest sense, the leaders of the church councils that discussed the issue of what books belonged in the Bible, right up to the Council of Carthage in 397 A.D., just did no more than a produce clerk does when he sorts out the boxes of apples, oranges, grapes, bananas, and peaches delivered on the truck and puts them in the proper bins in the grocery store. They recognized and acknowledged what the books of the Bible said for themselves.

Jesus, in Luke 11:51, identified the correct books of the Old Testament. He spoke of two deaths–Abel and Zechariah. The death of Abel is recorded in Genesis, the first book of the Old Testament. The death of Zechariah was recorded in 2 Chronicles 24, which incidentally is the last book of the Hebrew Bible that was used in Jesus' day. It is also important to recognize that the last book of the New Testament records a closure to the canon of Scripture. In Revelation 22:18-19, it says we are not to add or take away anything from the scriptures given by God. God closed the Book in 90 A.D. when John wrote the Revelation.

The Fourth Issue: Is the Bible of Today Reliable?

We do not have any of the original manuscripts, so do we have a reliable Bible? Yes, for many reasons we can say we have the Word of God but none so important as Psalm 17:9 which says the Word of the Lord is perfect, sure, right, pure, clean, true and righteous. None of the evidences are so convincing as 1 Peter 1:25 which says, **The word of the Lord endureth forever.** I can imagine that gets us past the time of the apostles and on into eternity. But the skeptics abound and here is more evidence for those so foolish to not take it on faith. First, the scribes who copied the scriptures believed that if they intentionally made a mistake they would go to hell. All copies were checked by scribal readers who counted the letters and if the letters did not match the original number of a book then the job had to be done again until it matched. No book on the market today has ever been proofread so much as the Bible for errors. Second, we have over 27,000 manuscript copies, especially with the find of the Dead Sea Scrolls, wherewith we can check the accuracy of the Bible. We have manuscripts dating back to the second century A.D. which puts us real close to the time of the Bible. Elapsed time and multiple copies would be blamed for errors, but this argument fails with such ancient manuscripts. Third, Bible scholars who specialize in checking for Bible errors say that we have no more than 150,000 variants in the text when manuscripts are compared. They don't even call them errors. Why? Because, according to these experts, the changes in the copies centers around misspelled words, differences in word order, insertion, omission, or change of a word which does not change the meaning of the text one bit. While 150,000 variants sounds like a lot, when you consider that the Bible has 773,692 words this means there is only one copy change for every seven words. With multiple thousands of copies that have been made it is absolutely phenomenal that there are not more changes. The only changes that would introduce possible errors into the present modern day text are variants where whole phrases or sentences have been omitted or inserted. Turns out many of these are things that appear in Mark's gospel but are not in Matthew's gospel. All in all, these big changes amount to only 1/1000 of the Bible text. That is equivalent to half a page of paper.

Sir Fredric Kenyon, who served as the director of the British Museum for twenty-one years, a museum that houses some of the most significant ancient manuscripts of the Bible, is quoted as saying, "The Christian can take the whole Bible in his hand and say without fear or hesitation that he holds in it the true word of God, handed down without essential loss from generation to generation throughout the centuries." That is the miracle of Transmission of the Bible. It is almost more phenomenal than the translation of the Bible.

Men have died for it. Most men will not die for a lie. Archaeology has dug up evidence after evidence with every shovelful of dirt to prove the Word of God to be true. Prophecy has left no trace of error in the Bible with its constant prediction of events–108 separate prophecies of Christ's ministry alone fulfilled hundreds of years after they were predicted by the Old Testament. Science has proven the Bible to be infallible. The power of the words to save souls brands it the true Word of God. The process of translation guards it as the Word of God. The preservation of its very text verifies it as the Word of God. The archaeologists spade confirms it as the Word of God. My friend, if you cannot believe the Bible is true you cannot believe anything is true, and you have no hope whatsoever for anything good in your life. That is a fact!

Reflection Station:

1. If someone were to tell you that they believe the Bible is just a book written by man how would you answer them?

2. What is meant by the statement that the Bible is Verbally Inspired?

3. What were some of the guidelines for deciding what books belonged in the Bible as inspired Scripture?

4. How many words are in the Bible? ☺

The Doctrine of the Prayer

LESSON TITLE: The Doctrine of Prayer - Prostrateology

SCRIPTURE: Luke 11:1, Matthew 21:13, Luke 6:12, Luke 18:1, 1 Samuel 12:23, James 5:16-17

TRUTH TO GAIN: There is no greater grace to work on in the Christian life than prayer. Prayer was instituted by God for God to please man, not for man to please God. The tendency to doubt this reality is countered by the many spiritual mechanisms God has put in place for prayer to be successful in the believer's life.

The Greatest Hindrance to Prayer

If you had to guess what would you believe to be the greatest hindrance to prayer: selfishness, Satan, service, sickness, strife, sin, sleepiness, or self-sufficiency? The greatest hindrance to prayer is none of the above. The greatest hindrance to prayer is neglect. If the believer would not neglect prayer he/she could overcome all the problems that strike at the heart of prayer and a defeated Christian life. Maybe you have heard the story of the two Christians from different towns who ran into each other at a convention and as they were talking about their respective churches, one said to the other, "What night do you have prayer meeting at your church?"

The other fellow said, "Actually, we stopped having prayer meeting at our church."

The other one said, "What does the congregation think about that?"

The first guy said, "They don't know it yet."

Would it not be true in most churches that few would complain if prayer was done away with altogether? What if the preacher said, "We can do our praying at home in private and make better use of our time when we come together for worship?" Would there even be the first outrage at such a proposal? One preacher put a top ten prayer list in the bulletin, but two months after he stopped only one person had even brought it to his attention, and that was after the preacher mentioned it first.

The real question about prayerlessness is what causes it, and the truthful conclusion is that the neglect of prayer comes in direct proportion to how much we sense our need of God. Prayer is all about dependance on God. People who don't pray much show they do not have much dependance on God. People quickly tire of a duty but they will give long hours and tireless commitment to a devotion, something or Someone they love and need. Perhaps prayerlessness comes from a failure to understand what prayer really is and how it works. Prayer is not meant to be reserved for the operations of super saints. James 5:16-17 proves that by saying that since Elijah, the praying giant of the Old Testament, was a man of "like passions" as we are, then great results can come from the praying of all God's children who are righteous and fervent.

The dean of the Theology School of Southwestern Baptist Theological Seminary in 1978 was Huber Drumwright. He was a man of exemplary prayer life. In the preface of his book, Prayer Rediscovered, he wrote, "The doctrine of prayer is the integrating doctrine of the Bible, though at times it has been treated as an appendix to Bible truth." Drumwright was correct on two points. Much detail is given in the volumes of notable Systematic Theologies on Bibliology, Angelology, Christology, Demonology, Soteriology, but prayer doesn't even have a technical term so applied in these kinds of books and rarely commands a fifth of the pagination given to the more prominent subjects. You have great writers like Herbert Lockyer who included a chapter on prayer in his book, *All the Doctrines of the Bible*, but he only gave five pages to the subject in a book of nearly three hundred pages. Yet if you go back nearly 200 years in time to 1835 you discover a man like Edward McKendree Bounds who had an astounding history in prayer. He passed the bar exam at age 19 and practiced law till he was 24 when God dramatically called him to preach. E. M. Bounds arose at 4 o'clock each morning and prayed for three hours. Consequently he spent nineteen years of his life writing on intercessory prayer amassing an authorship of over ten volumes on prayer. It is safe to say that an author will not write much more than their own personal experience in prayer. Drumwright correctly observed that the integrating force for all the doctrines of the Bible would be prayer. The fall of man in Anthropology disturbs you till you study in Christology the call of Jesus Christ to be our High Priest. That work of His High Priesthood comes into amazing focus when you realize He died to earn the right of being our Intercessor who in Soteriology will save us to the uttermost. It is therefore fitting to bring to this volume on Foundational Doctrines of the Bible a study on prayer, correctly called Prostrateology.

Common Misunderstandings About Prayer

To misunderstand something is quite often the forerunner of misusing something. In a small county town the police officers still wrote their reports by hand, and the data was entered later by a computer tech into their database. One theft report stated that a farmer had lost 2,025 pigs. Thinking that to be an error, the tech called the farmer directly: "Is it true Mr. (Smith) that you lost 2,025 pigs?" she asked.

"Yeth," lisped the farmer.

The girl was enlightened and entered to the record: "Subject lost 2 sows and 25 pigs." It's a good thing that gal understood the farmer and set the record straight. The record really needs to be set straight about prayer.

We will discover later in this lesson how Jesus set the record straight about errors in our praying. He spoke of things like repeating yourself - "use not vain repetitions." He downplayed the prayers of men who prayed in public to be seen of men and said this was hypocritical as well as receiving no reward from heaven. All of this is taught in the Sermon on the Mount in Matthew 6. But there is a great insight to a misunderstanding about prayer in Luke 18. In that passage Jesus taught that **prayer is not wishful thinking**. Two characters take center stage in the story, the Pharisee and the Publican. Verse 11 says, **The Pharisee stood and prayed thus with himself, God, I thank thee, that I am not as other men are, extortioners, unjust, adulterers, or even as this publican.** The key phrase that pinpoints the error is "prayed thus with himself." The implication here is that this man's prayers did not even reach the ears or heart of God. The problem was that this Pharisee's attempt at praying was full of pride and personal gain. There is a lot that goes on in the name of praying that is not praying at all but only wishful thinking. Prayer is not talking with God about what we want, but talking with God about what He wants. The Publican prayed the right prayer and was justified because he was asking God for something that God wanted– to give mercy to a confessed sinner.

True praying is all about having such a daily relationship of intimacy with God that God can think His thoughts through us and accomplish His will on earth by our requests. When we go to God only in emergencies it testifies to God that we're more concerned with our desires than His. Quite often someone will say they would like to win a million dollars by playing the lottery. Someone with sense will say, "Oh, that is just wishful thinking." This is an accurate assessment because the lottery is not the prescribed method in the Word of God for how the Lord may bring a million dollars into our lives. It would be a sin to pray to win the lottery. Why? Wealth comes from God not through stealing dollars from all the losers in a lottery to make you rich. God has chosen to bring wealth into our lives through proper stewardship, hard labor, wise planning, and humility.

There are numerous passages in the Scripture to confirm that God wants to bless us through proper stewardship, hard labor, wise planning, and humility. You need to tithe to be a good steward or you are robbing God and God never prospers a thief. If you don't work hard like the ant in Proverbs 6, all the wishful thinking in the world will not stop your oncoming poverty. People need to plan well by laying up treasures in heaven, giving to the poor, and saving some instead of spending everything they get. Finally, if you don't realize that everything you have is a gift of God, the Giver may not trust you with much because He operates within the principle "thou hast been faithful over a few things; I'll make you ruler over much." Wishful thinking cannot erase or reverse a pattern of disobedience. So if prayer is not wishful thinking, what is it? Prayer is touching and agreeing with God to get His glorious will done in our lives.

Prayer is **not for the purpose of avoiding hardship**. It is perfectly alright to pray for hardship to pass but sometimes God's will is to give us grace to endure hardship. Paul prayed for a thorn in his side to be removed but God denied the request three times telling him that the

Lord's grace was sufficient to endure the thorn and God would be glorified in Paul's weakness (2 Corinthians 12). Even Christ in Gethsemane prayed for the cup of suffering, the cross, would pass but He said, **Nevertheless not as I will, but as thou wilt (Matthew 26:39).** In prayer we often make two errors concerning hardship. We pray to avoid it too quickly. Secondly, we pray too quickly to accept it. The confusion and frustration of how to pray is avoided if we learn to pray deliverance prayers when it is the attack of the enemy. Then secondly, we must pray submission prayers when the hardship is bringing about the purpose of God. Prayer must discern the will of God and be willing to accept that path no matter how hard it is.

The last misunderstanding about prayer is that **if prayer is secondary in our spiritual discipline we can still have a blessed Christian life**. Nothing could be further from the truth. The apostle Paul wrote in 1 Thessalonians 5:17, **Pray without ceasing.** Unceasing prayer is a command from God for the Christian life. The prophet Samuel told Israel, **God forbid that I should sin against the LORD in ceasing to pray for you (1 Samuel 12:23).** Prayerlessness is a sin, and a sin that leads to defeat, despair, and depression in the Christian life. The fact that there are 650 definite recorded prayers in the Bible, 450 of which have recorded answers, proves that God does not consider prayer to be secondary in our Christian life. God's son, Jesus, made it primary in His life. How strong are you in your prayer life? If you are not motivated in your prayer life do you know why? Prayer is called a spiritual discipline but it is better to call it a spiritual delight. It is not the discipline that motivates us to pray as much as it is the delight. Do you delight to be in the presence of God? Have you discovered His awesome and amazing goodness? The Psalmist wrote (34:8), **O taste and see that the LORD is good: blessed is the man that trusteth in him.** King David compared it to a deer that "panteth after the water books" in Psalm 42. How much do you thirst for God? Have you really found something in this life that is more worthy than God and consumes far more of your attention?

The Words That Are Important

The Bible has several words for prayer such as intercession, petition, supplication, confession, thanksgiving, praise and adoration. These are English words in the Biblical text that have translated thirteen words in

Hebrew and Greek for prayer. A look at each one will be valuable to discover how we can be effective in our praying.

The most common word in the Hebrew Old Testament for prayer is *palal*. It is used 156 times in the verb and noun form. The word has the idea of calling on God to act as a judge or a mediator in a situation that needs His assessment and intervention. In Psalm 17 David prays this kind of prayer to ask God to step in between him and his enemies. David affirms that he has not transgressed with his lips, and his heart has been proven to be true to God. However, David claims that his enemies have been like lions who lurk in secret places going all around him with deadly intentions. David is confident that God will judge the situation and show His lovingkindness to the faithful and knock down the enemies. This kind of prayer is called supplication in 1 Kings 8 where Solomon has built the great temple and stands before the altar to call on God to remember the Davidic covenant and keep watch day and night over the temple, dwelling with the people. *Palal* is confident praying that God truly cares about His people and will not forsake His cause among them.

The Hebrew word *atar* speaks of a spontaneous, emotional, and personal cries to God for help. In 1 Chronicles 5, the Israelite tribes east of the Jordan were in battle trouble and they cried out to God. Verse 20 says, **And they were helped against them, and the Hagarites were delivered into their hand, and all that were with them: for they cried to God in the battle, and he was entreated of them; because they put their trust in him.** The English word *entreated* is a common way this word is translated. Manasseh was a wicked king of Judah, probably the most wicked king of all that ruled. God sent him into Babylonian captivity. In 2 Chronicles 33:12-13 we read he had a change of heart.

> **And when he was in affliction, he besought the LORD**
> **his God, and humbled himself greatly before the God**
> **of his fathers, And prayed unto him: and he was**
> **entreated of him, and heard his supplication, and**
> **brought him again to Jerusalem into his kingdom.**
> **Then Manasseh knew that the LORD he was God.**

The word *entreated* is seen again. It means to be heard, touched, and moved. We can pray and see God bend down to show tender care for the undeserving. Entreated involves being touched in the spirit as well as well as hearing with the ear. Are you able to touch God in your praying?

Paga is another word in Scripture's prayer vocabulary. It speaks of "meeting" or "making contact with." The idea of intercession comes to play in this word. It is the picture of using one's influence on behalf of another. Quite often we will say, "That person can really get in touch with God." A true intercessor is not one who dabbles in prayer but daily and powerfully enters the prayer closet to do business with God. This is *paga*.

The Hebrew word *Shama* is a favorite of the Jews. In fact, every day in the synagogue the Hebrew *Shema* was read which is Deuteronomy 6:4, **Hear, O Israel: The LORD our God is one LORD.** In this case, it speaks of Israel hearing this profound truth about God: God is one God. *Shama* means to hear intelligently and attentively. Psalm 34:17 says, **The righteous cry, and the LORD heareth, and delivereth them out of all their troubles.** God will hear our prayers if sin doesn't stand in the way. He has a heart to hear the troubles of our heart.

Another word for prayer used much in the Old Testament is *sha'al*. It means to inquire, beg, or ask. When the request is made by a superior the word means to "demand." When the request is made by an inferior it means to "seek a favor." More often than not this word is used to talk about our asking God for guidance. Too many Christians head out into life without asking the guiding hand of God.

When one prays with intense emotion asking God for grace and kindness the Hebrew word that expresses this kind of praying is *tahanun*. Jeremiah 3:21 is an example: **A voice was heard upon the high places, weeping and supplications of the children of Israel: for they have perverted their way, and they have forgotten the LORD their God.** *Tahanun* is translated "supplications" in the text and is notably paired with weeping. Do you ever weep before God for the sins of others or your own. There is grace to receive for such intense praying.

Another good word in the Old Testament vocabulary of prayer is *baquash*. In Ezra 8, the priest was leading a team of builders back to Jerusalem to restore the city after the Babylonian captivity. Ezra was carrying three and three-quarter tons of silver and gold for the rebuilding.

He knew that he had enemies all around for the return trip. But Ezra had boasted to the king that God would take care of them, and said he was ashamed at that point to ask the king for a military escort. He calls a fast and tells the people to seek God for protection. Verse 8 perfectly describes the passion in this kind of praying:

> **Then I proclaimed a fast there, at the river of Ahava, that we might afflict ourselves before our God, to seek of him a right way for us, and for our little ones, and for all our substance.**

Baquash is translated "seek," and is accompanied with a strange behavior which few saints have familiarity in this age. They "afflicted themselves." The meaning of this "affliction" is not hidden as though it is a mystery, but actually indicated in the verse. The affliction was fasting. It is self-imposed restraint from the normal intake of food and drink to concentrate on God and His answer to this prayer. This kind of praying is striving in intercession to God for His blessings, a willingness to set aside necessary food for communion with God and the favor of God.

Finally, the Hebrew word *Ana* means for God to hear us when we pray. Psalm 4:1 says, **Hear me when I call, O God of my righteousness: thou hast enlarged me when I was in distress; have mercy upon me, and hear my prayer.** While there are other Hebrew words for prayer these are the primary words, and they all indicated that despite God's awesome nature of being so high above His creation He has constant concern for our welfare and will hear our prayers to save us from harm.

The New Testament has six basic words for prayer. *Proseuchomai* is found eighty-five times in the New Testament. Other forms of the word are *euchomai* and the noun form *proseuche*. This is a word which refers to steadfast, continual, intensive devotion to prayer. This is the word that shows that God is involved with every area of our life. It is the word used in the Model Prayer which boils it down to the central needs of our life.

Aiteo is the word for asking, requesting, or desiring something from God. This is the God who says if we ask him for bread He is not going to give us a stone, nor if we ask him for fish He will not give us a serpent. God cares for us. It is fitting to ask Him for things. He may not give us everything we ask of Him, but He never tells us not to ask unless we are asking amiss, or selfishly. This is the word for praying away worries in Philippians 4:6, **Be careful for nothing; but in every thing by prayer and supplication with thanksgiving let your requests be made known unto God.**

Deomai and *Deesis* are the New Testament words for when you pray in deep personal need, requesting and expecting God to help. In Luke 5 a leper came to Jesus one day and the Scripture says he fell on his face and besought him, implored Him to make him clean. This is the major Greek word which is translated "supplication." Supplication is making specific requests. In other words, we don't have to beat around the bush with God.

Eratao is the Apostle John's favorite word for prayer. This word is found sixty-two times in the New Testament, twenty-seven of which are in John's writings. The word is found in its most essential meaning when Luke 4:38 tells of Jesus coming to Simon Peter's mother-in-law to heal her of the fever. Luke says, "and they besought him for her." This implies an intimacy with the Lord upon which one may ask for special grace. This is the word used in the High Priestly prayer of Jesus in John 17, a prayer revealing great intimacy between the Son and the Father. How intimate are you with God?

One more word deserves mention in this great catalog of prayer words. *Boao* is the word used of the blind man on the Jericho road who cried out in a tumultuous, disturbing way for Jesus' healing hand. **And he cried, saying, Jesus, thou Son of David, have mercy on me (Luke 18:38).** It is also the word used for Christ's last cry on the cross to the Father before giving up the ghost. We can be assured that in our deepest distresses of life there is a God who stands so close to hear our most pitiful cries. Have you ever just wailed before God? There is a touch from heaven in that kind of praying, like no other time in our praying. Why do you think that God would have so many words for prayer in the Bible? Would that not be proof that He has given us many open doors to be sure we come to Him in all things? Prayer, truly is not secondary with God.

Learning From Christ About Prayer

There can be no higher example for the Christian life than the Savior of the world, Jesus Christ. In fact, there are two scriptures that urge us to take the pattern of his life and make it ours also. The very one who tried to follow Jesus with all of his heart but denied the Lord three times wrote in one of his epistles, **For even hereunto were ye called: because Christ also suffered for us, leaving us an example, that ye should follow his steps" (1 Peter 2:21).** Peter had failures in his life but he did not quit following Christ after his failures. We may struggle with prayer but we must not quit. Ephesians 5:1 says, **Be ye therefore followers of God, as dear children.** The word for "followers" in that text is literally "mimic." Duplicate it exactly is our instruction. Christ taught us in prayer both by word and example. His example backed up His word. He never failed to practice what He preached. Christ's verbal instruction about prayer can be found in passages such as Matthew 5-7, Luke 11, Matthew 17, Matthew 18:19-20, Mark 11:22-24, John 14:13-14, John 15:7-16, and John 16:23-24. But what about the personal practice of prayer in Jesus' life. Can we learn anything from that?

We learn from Christ's prayer life about **DEPENDENCY IN PRAYER.** Jesus said, **I can do nothing of myself" (John 5:19).** This is why Jesus' practice was to rise up before the dawn of the day and go into a secluded place like a mountain to have time with God. Prayer is showing your dependency on God. When you don't pray you prove you don't depend upon God and are self-sufficient. Dependency is not proven in times of despair. Dependency is proven in daily reliance upon God. Jesus taught us to pray, "give us this day our daily bread." It is not logical to ask for your daily bread at the end of the day. Psalm 5:3 says, **My voice shalt thou hear in the morning, O LORD; in the morning will I direct my prayer unto thee, and will look up.** Morning prayer indicates our total reliance upon God for strength, guidance, and provision as the day starts.

We learn from Christ's prayer life about the **FAITH FOR PRAYING.** Jesus had faith to heal the blind, the lame, the leper, and the dead. He put doubters out of the room when He healed Jairus' daughter. He taught that **And all things, whatsoever ye shall ask in prayer, believing, ye shall receive (Matthew 21:22).** It is impossible to please God in our prayer life without faith (Hebrews 11:6). James, the half brother of the Lord, taught, **But let him ask in faith, nothing wavering. For he that wavereth is like a wave of the sea driven with the wind and tossed. For let not that man think that he shall receive any thing of the Lord.** Faith is not persistent begging. It is unrelenting confidence in the promises of God. Faith doesn't quit until the object of that faith, known to be acceptable in the will of God, is received. One of my all-time favorite passages on prayer and faith is 1 John 5:14-15 which says, **And this is the confidence that we have in him, that, if we ask any thing according to his will, he heareth us: And if we know that he hear us, whatsoever we ask, we know that we have the petitions that we desired of him.** Have you learned to pray this way?

We learn from Christ's prayer life about **FASTING FOR POWER**. Jesus fasted for forty days and nights in the wilderness which gave Him the power to overcome the devil's temptations. When the disciples could not cast the demons out of a little boy Jesus told them that "this kind cometh not out but by prayer and fasting." Then Jesus cast the demons out and the boy was well. Because of fasting Christ was victorious. Fasting empties us of our own selfish cravings, purifies our mind in concentration on the will of God, and empowers us to face strong opposition to the purposes of God.

We learn from Christ's prayer life about the **EXCHANGE IN PRAYER**. Prayer was never a one-way conversation for Jesus. In the High Priestly prayer of John 17 Jesus says,

> **Now they have known that all things whatsoever thou hast given me are of thee. For I have given unto them the words which thou gavest me; and they have received them, and have known surely that I came out from thee, and they have believed that thou didst send me.**

Jesus heard from God in His prayer life, and spoke those things God told Him to say. The promise of Jeremiah 33:3 is still active: **Call unto me, and I will answer thee, and show thee great and mighty things, which thou knowest not.** The sweetest times in a believer's communion with God is to hear a word of comfort, a word of courage, a word of promise, a word of blessing, or a word of direction. God still assures His children, who will draw close to Him and listen, with a word of mighty peace to the soul. Prayer is our most valuable asset in the Christian life.

Reflection Station:

1.   What does the Bible mean when it says the Pharisee "prayed with himself?"

2.   Look over the Old Testament and New Testament words for prayer (pages 99-103) and discuss which ones are most helpful to your prayer life.

3.   Would you agree with the statement that says if we are neglecting prayer we show that we are not dependant upon God?

LESSON ELEVEN
The Doctrine of Prophecy

LESSON TITLE: The Doctrine of Prophecy - Eschatology

SCRIPTURE: 2 Peter 1:19, Isaiah 46:9-10, 1 Thessalonians 4:13

TRUTH TO GAIN: The study of Bible prophecy is essential for the believer in these last days to gain hope. The study of Bible prophecy is advantageous for the believer in these deceptive times to avoid false doctrine. The study of Bible prophecy in all times has been neglected for the wrong reasons, presuming that such study is too complex and controversial.

The Importance of Studying Prophecy

The major reason why Christians do not study prophecy, preachers do not preach and teach Bible prophecy, and Bible Colleges do not offer many electives on Bible Prophecy is the claim that Bible prophecy is complex and too controversial. The fact of the matter is that God did not write His Bible to divide Christians, even though such has happened through disagreements over interpretation of the Scriptures. Peter says we have a "sure" word of prophecy. The Greek word for "sure" is *bebaios*, and it speaks of a firm and steadfast base which holds things stable. Prophecy was not meant to be divisive but reinforcing and strengthening to the body of Christ.

If there is anything that Satan hates in all the doctrines, it is the doctrine of eschatology. Prophecy is history written in advance of its fulfillment. Prophecy predicts Satan's destruction. Therefore, he is most assuredly all about bringing confusion, rejection, and deception into Bible prophecy more than anything else we might study in the Word of God. Is that a reason to neglect it in order to stay safe from Satan's wiles? Absolutely not, for in so doing we fall into the very trap we are trying to avoid. Satan will not leave you alone just because you leave Bible Prophecy alone.

There are seven primary reasons why every Christian should love and study Bible prophecy. **Number One: Bible Prophecy occupies a large proportion of the Word of God.** There are 31,124 verses in the Bible. A full 8,352 of those verses are Bible Prophecy. That means twenty-seven percent of the Bible is prophecy. Would a woman have three kids and attend to the needs of two of them but totally neglect the third one? There are sixteen prophecy books in the Old Testament and four prophecy books in the New Testament. That is nearly one-third of the total sixty-six books in the Bible concentrating on prophecy. Evidently God loved it. So should we!

Number Two: Prophecy magnifies Jesus and His Word. This generation of skeptics doubts the truth of the Word of God and the reality of Jesus Christ as the Saviour of the world. There are over 300 prophecies in the Old Testament that were fulfilled to the exact detail in the first coming of Jesus Christ as the Messiah. These were things like being born in a specific town named Bethlehem, born of a virgin mother, living a sinless life, being numbered in death among criminals, being buried in a borrowed rich man's tomb, and rising from the dead on the third day. Things like riding in on a donkey to the exact day six hundred years after Daniel wrote the prediction staggers the imagination. The chances of Jesus fulfilling only eight of these prophecies is comparable to the odds of burying a hundred silver dollars across the State of Texas two feet deep, marking only one of them, and sending out a blindfolded man to try and find and dig up that marked silver dollar. God knows the end from the beginning according to Isaiah 46 and has given us an accurate Word and a perfect Savior for our trust.

Number Three: The study of Bible Prophecy will keep the Christian from being deceived by false cults, false doctrine, and false prophets. The prophetic passages of the New Testament tell us that in the latter days there will be escalated deception to the point that if it were possible even the very elect would be deceived. There will be doctrines of devils, seducing spirits, damnable heresies, and claims of false Christs. Bible prophecy exposes all this but ignorance of Bible prophecy leaves the Christian vulnerable to deception. Most cult members today have come from mainline denominations. That is because they weren't grounded in Biblical truth.

Number Four: The study of Bible Prophecy promotes an evangelistic church. The church of Thessalonica was an infant church but they were taught the principles of God's prophetic plan and they were one of the most evangelistic churches the Apostle Paul ever planted. In Acts 8 God told Phillip before it happened that if he would go to Gaza there would be an Ethiopian eunuch waiting there for him to explain Jesus. Phillip went on the prophetic word and a man got saved because of it. Paul used Old Testament prophetic scriptures that Jesus fulfilled to share the gospel with the Jews. Christians who expect the Lords' imminent return will work to reach others before it is too late.

Number Five: Bible Prophecy has a purifying effect on the believer's life. 1 John 3:3 says, **And every man that hath this hope in him purifieth himself, even as he is pure.** What hope? John was talking about the hope of the Second Coming of Jesus Christ. A bride gets ready for her wedding. She does not want to be filthy when the Bridegroom comes. That would be a shame and embarrassment to her. Many Christians today are caught up in materialism. This world has a hold on their hearts because they have shoved aside thoughts of the next world and Christ's return. Bible prophecy tells us these things will all be burned up. Bible prophecy tells us that someday our soul will be required of us and then "whose things will those things be." Bible prophecy teaches us to "abide in him; that, when he shall appear, we may have confidence, and not be ashamed before him at his coming."

Number Six: Bible Prophecy offers confident hope in dark times. 2 Peter 1:19 tells us that Bible Prophecy is that lamplight in dark days when Satan's kingdom is seeking to triumph over God's kingdom. Christians will suffer persecution. Christians will face deep trials in this life. Christians will be attacked and accused by the enemy. Bible Prophecy sounds a loud trumpet and says, "Look up for your redemption draweth nigh."

Number Seven: God Himself invites us to study Bible Prophecy. Isaiah 45:11 says, **Thus saith the LORD, the Holy One of Israel, and his Maker, Ask me of things to come concerning my sons, and concerning the work of my hands command ye me.** Revelation 1:3 says, **Blessed is he that readeth, and they that hear the words of this prophecy, and keep those things which are written therein: for the**

time is at hand. The only book of the Bible which pronounces a special blessing upon those who study it is a prophecy book, the book of Revelation. But quite often it is a neglected book. People are missing out on the blessing. Saints should read it. Teachers should teach it. Preachers should preach it. Churches should cherish it.

One of the reasons why Bible prophecy is neglected is the mystery that surrounds it and the disagreements that surface because of views of interpretation. There is a simple rule which will clear up the confusion. Prophecy study does not have to be so hard if the student will let God's Word speak for itself rather than trying to make it say something it never intended to say. Personal prejudices are the chief reasons why there is so much controversy surrounding Bible Prophecy. When people make up their mind that God could not have meant literally what He said they demonstrate their personal prejudice. The simple rule that solves this problem is: *When the simple sense of Scripture makes sense, seek no other sense, unless the context indicates otherwise.*

Bible prophecy is full of symbols. Students question whether the symbols are to be interpreted literally or figuratively. Is the thousand year millennium really a literal thousand years? Does the bottomless pit really have no bottom? Are the candlesticks, angels, stars, and beasts of Revelation symbolic or literal and real? You can count on the Scripture to tell you nearly every time when the symbol in a passage represents something else. Otherwise prophecy needs to be taken literally to understand it correctly. In this lesson we will look at the major future events of prophecy which outlines God's plan for man.

Death and The Intermediate State

The oldest announcement of prophecy is the promise of death for men. It is a six-thousand-year-old announcement. Hebrews 9:27 only repeats what God said in Genesis 2:17. It is appointed unto man once to die because God clearly warned the first sinners, **But of the tree of the knowledge of good and evil, thou shalt not eat of it: for in the day that thou eatest thereof thou shalt surely die.** Death has passed upon all men according to Romans 5:12. So according to Bible prophecy the only thing that will forego the experience of death for believers is the Rapture. Unbelievers have no hope at all to escape death regardless of when the Rapture happens. Despite the unpleasant nature of the subject of death, its certainty demands we look at the issues and reality of our earthly tabernacle's end.

First of all, **death is not the end of our existence.** The oldest book in the Bible states the case. **But man dieth, and wasteth away: yea, man giveth up the ghost, and where is he (Job 14:10)?** For Job, the place of existence beyond death was called Sheol. This word is found sixty-six times in the Hebrew and translates to such English words as grave, pit, death, and hell. The Bible student needs to realize that progressive revelation is the way God has worked with His people. The Old Testament saints did not understand about the distinctive places called heaven and hell. Sheol, to the Jewish mind, was the realm of the dead for both righteous and unrighteous. Sheol was a dark abode, a dismal, depressing place, a holding room of departed spirits before they went to be with God. This is why David wrote in Psalms 18:5, **The sorrows of hell (Sheol) compassed me about: the snares of death prevented me.**

All the way back to the first century A.D., the Jews taught that there were two compartments in Sheol: one which was a place of torment for the unrighteous, and Abraham's bosom, a place of comfort for the righteous. Sometime during the Medieval Ages, Bible teachers claimed that passages like Ephesians 4:8-10 and 1 Peter 3:19, where it speaks of Jesus descending into the "lower parts of the earth," "leading captivity captive," and "preaching unto the spirits in prison," were an explanation of two compartments of Hades. The New Testament words for hell is Hades, Gehenna, and Tartarus. So Hades which is the same as Sheol, according to these teachers, was made up of a place of torment for the unrighteous called Gehenna, and a place of comfort called Abraham's bosom. The claim is that Jesus went to hell and took out those Old Testament righteous saints and led them up to paradise. There really is no clear Scripture to prove such thinking.

It is true that sometimes the Old Testament writer thought of Sheol as a dismal place, but David writes in Psalm 16:10-11 that he fully expected after death that God would not leave his soul in hell (Sheol-the grave) to see corruption, but would show him the path to heaven; and he would enjoy pleasures forevermore at the right hand of God. There is really no reason to ever believe that the righteous stayed at any place after death but heaven. They immediately went into the presence of God. According to Luke 16, after death you will have a conscious existence. You will be able to see, hear, talk, and feel. You will also have a body which is recognizable. The rich man in hell recognized Lazarus. The believing thief on the cross was promised by Jesus to be with Him that day. Paradise had to be heaven, the eternal home of the redeemed in the presence of God the Father.

Second of all, **death has no sting for the believer**. This is definitively stated in 1 Corinthians 15:

> **So when this corruptible shall have put on incorruption, and this mortal shall have put on immortality, then shall be brought to pass the saying that is written, Death is swallowed up in victory. O death, where is thy sting? O grave, where is thy victory? The sting of death is sin; and the strength of sin is the law. But thanks be to God, which giveth us the victory through our Lord Jesus Christ (verses 54-57).**

The unbeliever's eternal state will be unrelenting pain of both body and soul. Jesus said, **Fear him who can destroy both body and soul in hell (Matthew 10:28).** But the believer will pass through the door of death, over the chilly waters of Jordan as the songwriter has so named it, with an angelic escort, and into the presence of God with the ease of simply going to sleep. We don't have the luxury now of asking those who've made the journey "how was it to die," but when we get there we will be confirmed in what we believe now, trusting God's word to be the joyful promise for the believer.

Finally, it must be gravely clear that according to Scripture **death is never reversed.** There is a fascination in our day with afterlife testimonies, out- of-the-body experiences, and near-death experiences. Book after book has been written on the subject, and the surprising thing is believers in Christ have swallowed the bait of Satan on this subject. The enemy would just as sure desire our confusion and undue concentration on the mystery of death rather than the mission of life. He delights in mesmerizing the mind with the occupation of the unknown rather than let us concentrate on the gospel enterprise of winning souls to get them ready for heaven. Nothing would delight the devil any more than to put *90 Minutes in Heaven*, written by a Baptist preacher, on how he was killed in a automobile collision and went to heaven for 90 minutes, but in actuality he only stood outside the gates of heaven and never got to see God. Lazarus of Bethany (John 11) has a better story. He died for three days but came back. But Lazarus didn't write a book about it. John told the story in one chapter to glorify the Resurrection and the Life. You may be saying, "Well Paul died and went to heaven and came back." No, he didn't. He says clearly in 2 Corinthians 12 that he did not know whether he was in the body or out of the body. You just cannot say Paul died when Paul didn't know that himself. He just says the man he knew (presumedly himself) was caught up to the third heaven. In addition Paul was forbidden to write about it. The "heaven and back" stories have become a cottage industry in Christendom, but they do not square with the Bible.

The Southern Baptist Convention in June 2014 adopted a resolution on the sufficiency of Scripture for understanding the afterlife. That resolution warned Christians not to allow "the numerous books and movies purporting to explain or describe the afterlife experience" to "become their source and basis for an understanding of the afterlife." This came after the sensational Todd Burpo story was made into the blockbuster film, *Heaven is for Real*, but later discovered to be a hoax by Todd's own confession. We should trust the Bible far more than any person's testimony despite the persecution we might bear of being accused to be haters and incompassionate.

Rapture and The Judgment Seat of Christ

The critics of the Rapture claim foremost that the word does not appear in the Bible. But the words trinity, depravity, deity, and Millennium are not in the Bible, yet Christians believe in all four. The idea of a Rapture comes from several passages in the Bible not the least of which is 1 Thessalonians 4:17, **Then we which are alive and remain shall be caught up together with them in the clouds, to meet the Lord in the air: and so shall we ever be with the Lord.** The words "caught up" translates the Greek word *harpazo*. It is the same word that is used in Acts 8:39 which says that Phillip was "caught away" to Azotus, some thirty miles away, after he baptized the Ethiopian eunuch. Phillip, in essence, had a horizontal rapture. He was snatched immediately from Gaza and taken to Azotus.

Now, those who deny the Rapture say that those who believe in it believe in two Second Comings of Jesus. That is not true. Premillennialists believe in two phases of the Second Coming, called the Rapture and the Revelation, because there is no way to harmonize the Scripture in seeming contradictions when it speaks of Christ's coming again. For example, in 1 Thessalonians 5:2 it says the Lord will come as a thief in the night, but in Revelation 1:7 it says every eye shall see him. In 1 Thessalonians 4:17 it says that believers will be caught up to meet the Lord in the air, but in Zechariah 14:4 it says that the Lord will come and his feet will stand on the Mount of Olives. The only way to harmonize these differences is to accept the fact of a Rapture which takes the Church out of this world before the 7 years Tribulation and before the Revelation of Jesus Christ at the last phase of the Second Coming.

The Rapture will involve only believers, dead or alive. Those believers who have gone to sleep in Jesus, their bodies buried and their souls with the Lord, will be resurrected first out of the ground and the corruptible body will be made incorruptible. Then according to 1 Thessalonians 4:17, the believers that are still alive when the Lord comes in the clouds will be changed in their bodies, given a body that is fit for heaven, and caught up in the clouds to be with the Lord and all the other believers who got out of the ground first. What a glorious day that will be!

Immediately after the Rapture God will judge believers at what is called the Judgment Seat of Christ. The Greek word for this is *BEMA*. Some scholars say this judgment will occur in the air but several factors in God's word indicate it will be in heaven. Since the Rapture happens in the twinkling of an eye (1 Cor. 15:52) it would be impossible for this event to occur as a thief in the night if the world could see us being judged in the air.

Secondly, the word *bema* is also translated throne. The scriptures portray all judgment coming from the throne and specifically under the authority of Jesus Christ, who is seated at the Father's right hand. It is essential that believers know that this Judgment Seat of Christ is not a judgment of their sins but of their works for Christ. Salvation of a man's soul comes when he puts his faith in Christ, who was judged for our sins two thousand years ago. If the Judgment Seat of Christ were a judgment of our sins the work of Calvary would be meaningless. No sins other than the valueless works we've done will ever be mentioned at the BEMA. Those sins have been separated as far as the east is from the west, and God remembers them no more according to Psalm 103:12 and Hebrews 10:17.

The Judgment Seat of Christ is a judgment of rewards for faithful work to Christ, giving them crowns to lay at the feet of Jesus for honor and granting them ruling and reigning positions in God's Millennial earth. Revelation 20:6 says, **Blessed and holy is he that hath part in the first resurrection: on such the second death hath no power, but they shall be priests of God and of Christ, and shall reign with him a thousand years.** There is no "shame and everlasting contempt" in the Judgment Seat of Christ (See Daniel 12:2).

The Seven Years Tribulation

For many reasons the Church will not go through the seven years Tribulation Period. First of all, this time is referred to in Jeremiah 30:7 as the "time of Jacob's trouble." The Tribulation period is a time for God to judge Gentile nations in their rebellion against God and persecution of Israel. This time is also called in Revelation 6 the "great day of the wrath of the Lamb." Christians have escaped that wrath by grace through faith.

When Paul discusses this Day of the Lord, which begins with the Tribulation Period, he writes in 1 Thessalonians 5:9, **For God hath not appointed us to wrath, but to obtain salvation by our Lord Jesus Christ.** That is consistent with the promise to the Philadelphian church in Revelation 3:10, **Because thou hast kept the word of my patience, I also will keep thee from the hour of temptation, which shall come upon all the world, to try them that dwell upon the earth.** Titus 2:13 says believers look for that **blessed hope and glorious appearing of the great God and our Saviour Jesus Christ.** What blessed hope would it be for the Bridegroom to leave the Bride in a world that will be so bathed with the wrath of God that two-thirds of mankind will die of plagues, and all Christians during that period will be martyred for their faith because they won't take the mark of the beast? The blessed hope is Jesus coming to snatch His church out before the Tribulation ever starts.

The Tribulation Period of seven years is divided into two parts– forty-two months each. The latter half is called the Great Tribulation. In the first half the seal judgments are broken and poured out on the earth causing one-fourth of the population of earth to die of starvation, plagues, war, and natural disasters. There will be destructive meteor showers in the sixth seal. Man will be frightened to the point of running into caves to hide, begging to die. In the second half of the Tribulation the trumpet judgments and bowl judgments will take the lives of one-third of the population by poisoned waters, deprivation of oxygen due to destruction of trees and grass, shipwrecks on bloody seas, freezing temperatures because of destruction to the sun, not to even mention the madness of men's minds when the demons are let out of hell to sting them. Who in their right mind would want to stick around on earth for this horror?

When does the Tribulation start? Many people ask today if we are not already in the Tribulation. That question would be laughable if it were not so pathetically ignorant. Number one, the Tribulation is described by Jesus in the Olivet Discourse of Matthew 24:21, **Such as was not since the beginning of the world to this time, no, nor ever shall be.** Anybody can read Revelation 6-18 and know full well that earth has not yet experienced these kinds of judgments at any time in her history. Secondly, visit the cemeteries and see if there has been a great unearthing of believer's bodies who've gone missing in the Rapture. According to 2 Thessalonians 2:3-10, there has to be a great "falling away,"literally apostasy from the faith, and then the removal of the restraining work of the Holy Spirit, before the Antichrist can appear. The Tribulation cannot start without the Antichrist. According to Daniel 9:24-27, the start of the 70th week for Israel, which is that last seven years of Tribulation, starts with the Antichrist, called the Prince, confirming a covenant of peace with Israel. He cannot come on the scene till the Church is taken out of the way, the church age being the dispensation of the work of God's Spirit, and a great apostasy of the faith happening on earth.

The Antichrist will have complete rule over the whole world during this time. If you don't take the mark of the beast you will not be able to buy or sell. If you don't starve to death you will be killed by the Antichrist, literally beheaded. Don't wait to become a Christian after the Church is Raptured. Towards the end of the Tribulation there will be several battles involving Russia, Egypt, armies from the east such as China and Japan, and the Antichrist's armies fighting against Jerusalem. At this point Jesus Christ will come again and consume them all with the words of His mouth. There in the Valley of Esdraelon in the mountains of Megiddo, a vast plain of 280 square miles, roughly three-fourths the size of Putnam County Tennessee, will be the site of the battle called Armageddon. The outcome of that battle will be so bloody it will run the depth of a horse's bridle. (See Revelation 14:20).

Why does God allow the Tribulation? He does it for three reasons. The wickedness of man must be punished. Secondly, it proves God is not silent or impotent. Critics shake their finger at God claiming He does nothing about evil. The Tribulation proves that not so. Thirdly, God will save a remnant of believing Jews through the Tribulation Period and a vast crowd of Gentiles according to Revelation 7. God will have His day of wrath.

The Second-Coming of Christ

Such delight must come to the Christian when he reads Hebrews 9:28, **So Christ was once offered to bear the sins of many; and unto them that look for him shall he appear the second time without sin unto salvation.** It has been over 5,500 years since God first told Moses, **That then the LORD thy God will turn thy captivity, and have compassion upon thee, and will RETURN and gather thee from all the nations, whither the LORD thy God hath scattered thee (Deuteronomy 30:3).** Jews from all over the world will return to their native land and God will prosper them. All the armies of the earth and Satan's Antichrist will be gathered against God and the Jews.

Revelation 19:11-21 tells us that Jesus Christ Himself will ride a white horse to earth with the armies of heaven. He will destroy all the enemies with the sword of His mouth. There will be so much carnage of dead people at that time that all the vultures of the world are called to that area to eat their fill. Jude 1:14-15 says, **Behold, the Lord cometh with ten thousands of his saints, To execute judgment upon all, and to convince all that are ungodly among them of all their ungodly deeds**

which they have ungodly committed, and of all their hard speeches which ungodly sinners have spoken against him. One day sinful man will be shut up and shut out because the King of Kings is coming, and if you're not in His kingdom you'll be judged worthy of eternal death.

The first coming of Christ was rejected. The Second Coming of Christ will be honored. He will rule with a rod of iron (Revelation 19:15). The only subject mentioned more frequently than the Second Coming in the New Testament is the subject of salvation. The Second Coming is mentioned eight times more frequently than the first coming of Christ. Christ's Second Coming is mentioned 318 times in the New Testament, which is more than all the chapters of the New Testament (216). Zechariah 12:10 says the Jews will have their eyes opened when Christ comes back, and they will mourn for him because they will realize they crucified their Messiah at His first advent. The whole purpose of the Second Coming is to fulfill what Christ taught us to pray, "thy will be done on earth as it is in heaven."

The Millennium

There are two major questions that are asked about the Millennium. Is it going to be a literal one thousand years and how will the Millennium be populated if resurrected people do not have children? The answers are found in Scripture. The first question can be dealt with quickly. In Revelation 20 the word "thousand" is used six times. It would be strange for God to have meant this symbolically rather than literally when he puts it in the passage six times. The critics who have a problem with a literal thousand years have no problem with a literal seven years Tribulation. It is safe to say that God knows what He means by His numbers. There is no symbolic interpretation satisfactory for the thousand year Millennium.

There will be ideal conditions on earth during the Millennium. The first condition will be **worldwide peace**. The world clamors for peace today but can't find it though many opposing leaders have gathered time and again to discuss the prospects. Since the fall of man we have been given to war, not peace. The world will not know true peace till the Prince of Peace comes. Isaiah 2:4 says at that time, **He shall judge among the nations, and shall rebuke many people: and they shall beat their swords into plowshares, and their spears into pruninghooks: nation**

shall not lift up sword against nation, neither shall they learn war any more.

The King of Kings will bring **health and prosperity** in the Millennium. Isaiah 35:5-6 says, **Then the eyes of the blind shall be opened, and the ears of the deaf shall be unstopped. Then shall the lame man leap as an hart, and the tongue of the dumb sing: for in the wilderness shall waters break out, and streams in the desert.** Isaiah 29:18 says that people will hear the words of the book and suddenly the blind eyes that have been dark will be opened with light and beautiful vision. There will be joy, and happiness, and sudden bursts of excitement in the thrilling blessings of this wonderful kingdom on earth. Hospitals will go out of business and insurance premiums will be a thing of the past. In fact, the health of mankind will be so good that original longevity of life will be restored and a person who dies at 100 years old will be considered an infant. Isaiah 65:20 says, **There shall be no more thence an infant of days, nor an old man that hath not filled his days: for the child shall die an hundred years old; but the sinner being an hundred years old shall be accursed.**

Thirdly, the Millennium will be characterized by **overwhelming knowledge of God**. One of the sweetest verses on this prospect is Isaiah 11:9 which says, **They shall not hurt nor destroy in all my holy mountain: for the earth shall be full of the knowledge of the LORD, as the waters cover the sea.** Every school will be a Bible School. Every home will be a seminary. In the halls of government there will be no place you can walk to where you cannot see a Bible. Everywhere you go on the streets people will not be talking about the weather, the economy, drugs, murder, riches, pleasure, or fame. They will be talking about Jesus, the Dayspring and the Lawgiver. The dark corners of rebellion will be few and far between and all uncovered to bow at His feet and proclaim Him King. He will be worshiped far and wide. Isaiah 66:23 says, **And it shall come to pass, that from one new moon to another, and from one Sabbath to another, shall all flesh come to worship before me, saith the LORD.** All that won't worship Him will be destroyed and laid in a public garbage heap where hordes of maggots eat their bodies and every passerby is astonished and shaken. (Isaiah 66:24)

Fourthly, **righteousness and holiness** characterizes the Millennium. There will be no abortion clinics. Planned Parenthood will be out of business. Newspapers will have no murders or mayhem to report. Isaiah 11:3-5 says,

> **... and he shall not judge after the sight of his eyes, neither reprove after the hearing of his ears: But with righteousness shall he judge the poor, and reprove with equity for the meek of the earth: and he shall smite the earth with the rod of his mouth, and with the breath of his lips shall he slay the wicked. And righteousness shall be the girdle of his loins, and faithfulness the girdle of his reins.**

He will not so much as let a wolf lick his bloodthirsty lips over a juicy lamb but will command the beast to lay beside the prey in submission. Even the animals will respect the holiness of God.

Finally, the Millennium will be a time of **fullness of the Holy Spirit** everywhere you look. Isaiah 44:3 is just one of those passages commenting on the flow of the Spirit during that age. **For I will pour water upon him that is thirsty, and floods upon the dry ground: I will pour my spirit upon thy seed, and my blessing upon thine offspring.** There will be no spiritual apathy, spiritual coldness, spiritual harlotry and worldliness. The love of God, fellowship of the saints, and power for preserving Christ's way will be at a fever pitch. Backsliders will have no place of comfort or excuse in those days.

How will the Millennium be populated? This question entertains a discussion of the sequence of resurrections indicated in Scripture. The saints in heaven will not be able to have children because they are not marrying or giving in marriage. There are four resurrections mentioned in Scripture. 1 Corinthians 15:23-24 says,

> **But every man in his own order: Christ the firstfruits; afterward they that are Christ's at his coming. Then cometh the end, when he shall have delivered up the kingdom to God, even the Father; when he shall have put down all rule and all authority and power.**

Christ was the first resurrection. "Afterward" does not mean immediately afterward because Paul uses the Greek word (*epeita*) that signifies a lapse of time of undesignated duration, and so those that are Christ's, i.e. saints, will come sometime later. This passage teaches us that the resurrections come by ranks, *tagma* in Greek which means companies of troops. Now, Revelation 20:4 tells us the Tribulation martyrs are resurrected at the Second Coming before the Millennium, after the Tribulation is over. So the Church Age saints are resurrected at the Rapture and the Tribulation saints are resurrected at the outset of the Second Coming before the Millennium.

When are the Old Testament saints resurrected? For that answer we go to Daniel 12:1-2,

> **And at that time shall Michael stand up, the great prince which standeth for the children of thy people: and there shall be a time of trouble, such as never was since there was a nation even to that same time: and at that time thy people shall be delivered, every one that shall be found written in the book. And many of them that sleep in the dust of the earth shall awake, some to everlasting life, and some to shame and everlasting contempt.**

The resurrection of Daniel's people, the Old Testament saints, comes at the time when Michael stands up against the Antichrist. That is at the end of the Tribulation. Then Revelation 20:5 says, **The rest of the dead lived not again until the thousand years were finished.** So there would be no way to populate the Millennial kingdom unless some unresurrected people enter the Millennium.

Ezekiel 20:38, Micah 2:12-13, Matthew 25:32-34, and Revelation 12:6,14 are passages that indicate there will be a Jewish remnant who will be protected in the wilderness of Bozrah. Zechariah 13:8-9 says only one-third of the Jews will make it. The rest will be killed by the Antichrist. At the end of the Tribulation and at the sight of Jesus coming in the clouds to Jerusalem, the Jews will mourn for Him and be saved in one day according to Zechariah 13:1. **In that day there shall be a fountain opened to the house of David and to the inhabitants of Jerusalem for**

sin and for uncleanness. For Israel, the constant sacrifices and Day of Atonement was only a brutal reminder of their sin. They need to see the fountain of Christ's bleeding hands, feet, and side to cover their sins.

The present world Jewish population is 13.3 million. If the salvation of Israel were to happen today it would mean over four million Jews would be saved in one day. Are there any others that will enter the Millennium that can have babies? Gentiles who survive the Tribulation have a chance to be saved and Revelation 7 says there will be a great host of them saved. Matthew 25 says Jesus will come and judge the sheep and the goats at the end of the Tribulation. Joel 3:2 says this will happen in the Valley of Jehoshaphat. The surviving sheep of the Gentile population will also enter the Millennium in redeemed but unresurrected bodies to be the parents of that new generation.

The most important question about the Millennium is what purpose does God have for it? There are two primary purposes. First, the fulfillment of all the covenants that God has made with Israel will be accomplished in the Millennium. In the Abrahamic covenant God will restore Israel to her glory, return the land to her possession, and bless the nations of the earth through her for a thousand years. In the Davidic covenant God will put the rightful heir on the throne of David, and Daniel (4:34) as well as Isaiah (9:7) says it will be an everlasting dominion with no end. In the New Covenant of Jeremiah 31, God will give believing Israel a new heart erasing their blindness.

The second purpose of the Millennium is to broadcast the real reason for man's rebellion against God. Revelation 20:3 says that Satan will be locked up in the pit for the thousand years. Christ will rule the world in righteousness every day of the Millennium. Thus if two of the evil influences in man's heart against God are dismissed during the Millennium, namely the devil and the world, then the only thing left to corrupt man's heart is his own flesh. It is almost a return to the Paradise of Eden to prove man's heart. Will he obey or disobey in a perfect environment? His choice will determine his eternal state.

The Great White Throne Judgment

Many will disobey during the Tribulation and the Millennium. They will be destroyed. Then Revelation 20:5-15 reveals that at the end of the Millennium Satan will be loosed for a season to go out and deceive the nations into final rebellion. The result will be deadly. All the bodies of unbelievers, those who died before the Tribulation, during the Tribulation, and during the Millennium will be resurrected and they will stand before the Great White Throne Judgment. It is a judgment of the works of sin in the unbelievers' hearts, and a final display that their names are not in the Lamb's Book of Life proving they are worthy of being cast alive into the lake of fire along with the devil, the Antichrist, the False Prophet, and all the devil's demons.

Several times in the Scriptures there is a reference to the nature of the unbeliever's judgment. John 5:29 calls it a review of evil and a resurrection to damnation. Daniel 12:2 calls it a resurrection to "shame and everlasting contempt." That word contempt means an object that is continuously abhorred and rejected. If this is the case then why are there books of works opened as a guide for this judgment? That book is to prove by evidence that there is nothing good or bad in their life which merits heaven. Jesus reminded us in Matthew 7 that there will be those who will throw up their good works to God as an argument for worthiness. But Jesus will say, **I never knew you: depart from me, ye that work iniquity.** John Gill's Commentary on this passage says that although an omniscient God had knowledge of their person, He is saying in judgment, "I never made any account of you, as mine, as belonging to me; I never approved of you, nor your conduct; I never had any converse, communication, nor society with you, nor you with me."

No person at this Great White Throne Judgment will have their names in that second book, the Lamb's Book of Life. That is a book of relationship which unbelievers do not have with God. All sinners on that day will be without excuse because there is nothing in the fine print. It is all in big bold letters in the Word of God long before it ever happens. Make no mistake about the outcome of this Great White Throne. All who appear here will get the same sentence–the lake of fire. At this point God has already cast Satan, the Antichrist, the False Prophet, and the demons there, so they are waiting on the sinners to arrive in that place of ultimate misery. The report is, "the smoke of their torment ascendeth up for ever and ever."

The Eternal State

The last topic of Eschatology is the eternal state. What will things be like when God wraps up His plan and ushers in the ages of the ages? Eternity literally is translated from the Greek phrase *aionios tou aioniou*, which means "unto the ages of the ages." The state of eternity is described fourfold in Scripture: 1) There will be a new earth; 2) There will be new heavens; and 3) There will be a New Jerusalem; and 4) There will be a lake of fire. The new earth is described in 2 Peter 3:12 where the **heavens being on fire shall be dissolved, and the elements shall melt with fervent heat?** God promised that He would not destroy the earth ever again by water; but the promise of God is that He will purge this sin-cursed earth by fire. This does not happen during the seven years Tribulation although there will be many judgments which will reshape the earth. No, this happens at the end of the Millennium when God, by fire, reverses all the effects of sin's curse upon planet earth. The Millennium causes the earth to take a temporary vacation from sin's curse when you see the lion laying down with the lamb and the baby playing on the hole of a snake den. But the conflagration of fire will be God's way of cleansing and purifying this earth for eternal habitation.

There will be new heavens. All three of them will be new. The first heaven, which you see by day, will be rolled back as a scroll as the new day of eternity is dawning. The second heaven, which you see by night, will be dissolved according to 2 Peter 3:12 to reveal a new curtain of the universe fit for the drama of an eternally ruling King. Finally, the third heaven where God dwells will be renewed and will never ever be the dispensary of wrath from an angry God ever again.

How long will it take to get to that third heaven? If you were to travel the speed of light which is 186,000 miles per second you could be to the Moon in 1.5 seconds, to the planet Mercury in 4.5 minutes, to Jupiter in 35 minutes and 11 seconds because it is 367 million miles out. You could go to the planet Uranus, which is taken from the Greek word for heaven *ouranos*, in just a little over two hours, but at 1.5 billion miles out into space you still would not be in heaven. The last planet that we know about is Pluto. There may be a million more for all we know but to the farthest reaches of our solar system you could travel in billions of miles and you still would not be off the front porch of this universe. Yet, in resurrection bodies you will be able to travel the vast reaches of God's final order at the speed of thought. At the Rapture, in the time it takes for light to blink off the pupil of your eye, you will be in heaven. How is that possible? I don't know. You'll have to ask God if I don't get to Him first. But what you must know now is whether you are saved, ready for heaven, and preparing for that accountability before God when He comes for us.

Reflection Station:

1.   What percentage of Scripture is Bible Prophecy?

2.   What is the name for the Judgment Seat of Christ?

3.   According to Scripture what starts the Tribulation Period? (See Daniel 9:24-27)

4.   How long will the bodies of sinners lay in the ground before they are resurrected to stand at the Great White Throne Judgment?

5.   What are some of the characteristics of the Millennium?

"For the time will come when they will not endure sound doctrine; but after their own lusts shall they heap to themselves teachers, having itching ears; And they shall turn away their ears from the truth, and shall be turned unto fables."

2 Timothy 4:3-4

I Need Your Help

If you found *Foundational Doctrines of the Christian Faith* to be a highly informative book on Bible doctrine, there are others who would greatly benefit from your reference to this book. Would you consider going to the link below and posting a short, honest review on Amazon and/or any other bookseller where you may have purchased it to help me grow as a writer, and help me reach others with the message. Thanks for purchasing my book and recommending it to others through your review. If your church would like to obtain multiple copies of this book, contact the author at 1-931-858-3730. Thanks for your support to this ministry.

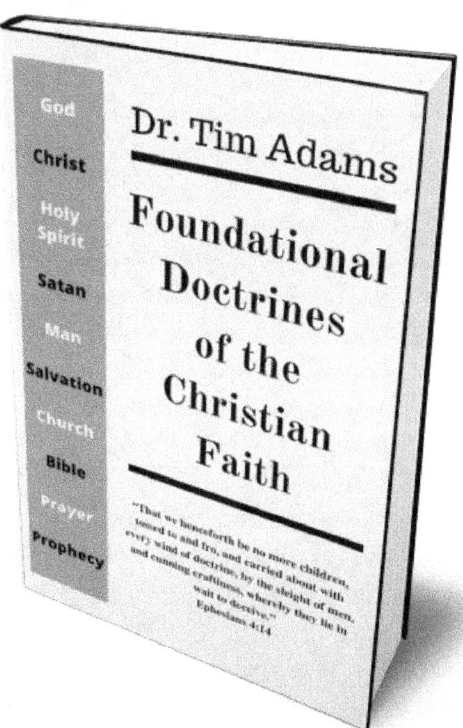

https://smarturl.it/FDBreview

More Books by Dr. Tim Adams

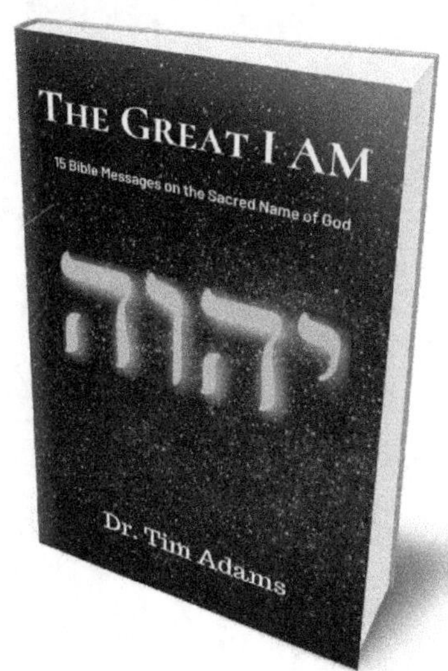

If you liked *It's Later Than You Think*, you may also enjoy reading other books by Dr. Adams.
Please check out my author page on Amazon.com.
Follow the link:
https://www.amazon.com/author/drtimadams

www.ingramcontent.com/pod-product-compliance
Lightning Source LLC
Chambersburg PA
CBHW052038150726
48002CB00002B/661